CONCISE AND UPD

TRUMPET BLAST WARNING

AN END TIME PROPHETIC WAKE UP CALL

JASON CARTER

Trumpet Blast Warning: An End Time Prophetic Wake Up Call
Concise and Updated Edition

Copyright © 2017 by Jason Carter.

No part of this book shall be reproduced or transmitted in any form or by any means, electronic or mechanical, including photocopying, recording, or by any information retrieval system without written permission from the publisher.

Published by Trumpet Blast Publishing and Branch Press.
For further copies of the concise and updated version email info@branchpress.com

For other titles by Branch Press visit www.branchpress.com

For copies of the unabridged version,
(500 page with photo section and extensive notes) visit:
www.trumpetblastwarning.co.uk or Amazon.

ISBN 978-1548499259

Special thanks to John Wright of
Branch Press for making this edition of
Trumpet Blast Warning available.

For other titles by Branch Press please visit
www.branchpress.com

During times of universal deceit, telling the truth becomes a revolutionary act.

George Orwell

Have nothing to do with the fruitless deeds of darkness, but rather expose them.

Ephesians 5:11 (NIV)

CONTENTS

1	A Heavenly Encounter	7
2	Mass Media, Mass Deception	9
3	The March towards World Government	11
4	Creating a Climate of Fear	15
5	Government Sponsored Terrorism	17
6	Disturbing Questions	19
7	The Final Empire	23
8	The Rise of the Antichrist	27
9	America Beguiled	31
10	Deception in the White House	35
11	The Secret Satanic Practices of the Global Elite	39
12	Freemasonry and the Illuminati	43
13	One World Religion	47
14	The Mark of the Beast	53
15	Surveillance Society	57
16	Tribulation Rising	61
17	The Migrant Crisis	65
18	World War Three	71
19	Countdown to the Apocalypse	75
20	Action Stations	79
21	We Will Not Fear	81
	Notes	83

Chapter 1

A HEAVENLY ENCOUNTER

In 2009 I had a dream. I felt myself lifted up out of my house, where I lay horizontally in the sky. Then a pair of hands appeared that placed something in my right side before I descended again to my bed.

I woke up, wondered what was happening to me, and fell asleep. I found myself in a bright room and came into the presence of God. An angel appeared who asked God what he should say to me. Then he put his left hand on my back and his right hand on my heart and spoke only one word – LOVE!

The next morning, when I awoke, I heard the Holy Spirit say, 'Will you not tarry with me for one hour?' I then had a most precious time of communion with God, followed by days seeking God for an understanding of the dream.

At that time the European Union was ratifying the Lisbon Treaty that would come into force in January 2010. But as I waited on God I experienced an increasing sense of danger regarding the EU and the woeful consequences of Britain's further integration.

At the same time the Lord reminded me of an earlier vision I had received in 1991 about the Maastricht Treaty, told in my book *Beyond Earthly Realms*.

On Sunday, five days after my dream, I felt compelled to get on my knees and prayed, 'Lord, give me a heart and a spirit like Daniel. Do not let me bow down to any ungodly world system or power.'

Instantly joy and peace flooded my soul.

When I got to Church, listening to our worship leader singing, I saw again the hands in my dream, but this time I saw that they placed six letters inside me. I knew I had to write urgently a warning to Her Majesty the Queen, Gordon Brown, then Prime Minister, and David Cameron, Leader of the Opposition.

I still had three letters to write. Then in January 2012 came the amendment to the Lisbon Treaty because of the problems of the Euro currency. I felt compelled to write the fourth letter, now contained in *Trumpet Blast Warning*.

In all this I was so conscious of Daniel, who received a touch from God and was told, 'O Daniel, greatly beloved.' I had also received a touch from God with that one word, 'LOVE.' Daniel had to be sure of the Love of God before he could transmit the plans of God. Intimacy with God is the true foundation for prophecy.

Since then I know that God is warning about calamitous times ahead, but also His passionate love for the world and His longing for everyone to know him before it is too late.

'Therefore keep watch, because you do not know on what day your Lord will come' (Matthew 24:42).

'He who has an ear, let him hear' (Revelation 3:20).

Chapter 2

MASS MEDIA, MASS DECEPTION

'By skilful and sustained use of propaganda, one can make a people see heaven as hell, or a most wretched life as paradise.' [1]

Adolf Hitler

Mass Media refers to reaching vast numbers of people electronically or in print. Propaganda is the transmission of information, often deceptive, that advances a political cause. Believing all that is said in the mass media is folly. After propaganda got a bad name under Hitler, it was re-branded by Edward Bernays as 'Public Relations'.

Bernays' work on how to control the masses was used by the Nazis to control Germany. The masses have a small intelligence and a great capacity to forget. The key is to repeat a few slogans endlessly until the public understands.[2]

After the last war, William Colby, a former CIA Director, said that the CIA owns everyone of any significance in the major media.[3] In 2012 the BBC was accused of being the European Union's propaganda arm after it admitted receiving £3 million in EU grants and a £141 million loan from the European Investment bank.[4]

In 1969 scientist Herbert Krugman found that in less than a minute watching television, brain waves move from Beta waves – active logical thought – to Alpha waves that are meditative and open to suggestion, as in hypnosis. Television is therefore an effective means for deceiving the masses through the transmission of propaganda.

We are warned that in the end days people will perish because they refused to love the truth and so will live under a powerful spirit of delusion. (2 Thessalonians 2:10-11). Television is a weapon of mass mind control paving the way for a tyrannical world government.

STOP PRESS

Since the rise of populism in the West, propaganda has accelerated to absurd levels. Today a panicked mainstream media brazenly reveals its bias toward the establishment.

We are bombarded minute-by-minute with anti-populist propaganda. So also Hollywood and the music industry have shown unfettered allegiance to the system. Movie stars and singers come out in force to sway the public mind in favour of the establishment. Dan Gainor, vice president of business and culture for the Media Research Center said; "Hollywood tried desperately to set the agenda for the 2016 election. It's no surprise they will try harder in 2017 to write the script for America."[5]

The war on 'fake news' is merely a means to justify increased censorship. Those calling for it are working to create a government-sanctioned "gatekeeper" with the power to shut down anyone who speaks against the political establishment. Hate speech, cyber bullying, fake news, conspiracy theory and 'Russian propaganda' are all labels being used by the establishment to stop opposing information being shared online. Chinese-style internet censorship has begun.

Chapter 3

THE MARCH TOWARDS WORLD GOVERNMENT

'Individual rights will be willingly relinquished for the guarantee of their well-being granted by the World Government.' [1]

Henry Kissinger, Secretary of State to President Nixon

Many have desired to rule the world, from Babylon to Rome, from Napoleon to Adolph Hitler. Now we are threatened by a new world government under the guise of groups such as the secretive Bilderberg Group, founded by Joseph Retinger, a politician and 33rd degree mason, who assemble annually the elite of the western nations.

David Rockefeller said in June 1991, thanking Media Moguls who attended Bilderberg meetings for their discretion, 'It would have been impossible to develop our plan for the world if we had been subject to the lights of publicity during those years. But the world is (now) more sophisticated and prepared to march towards a world government.'

Investigative journalist Daniel Estulin, in his book *The Bilderberg Group*, reveals that the Bilderberg Group want to destroy national sovereignty through subversion and control people by artificially manufactured crises that persuade people to give up rights to obtain security.[2]

Leaked papers from the 1955 Bilderberg Conference confirm their involvement in establishing the European Union and the Euro currency. Etienne Davignon, a former President of the European Commission and a former Chairman of the Bilderberg Group, later admitted this[3].

Other plans have been to form a North American Union of Canada, USA and Mexico with a single currency called the Amero[4]. In 2005, the Security and Prosperity Partnership was signed by President Bush, Paul Martin of Canada and Vincente Fox of Mexico[5].

Under such slogans as 'free trade' and 'environmental protection', nations surrender piece by piece their sovereignty to form regional governments. Lies were used to draw Britain into Europe. Edward Heath said in 1973 that, 'fears that the UK would lose independence and sovereignty are completely unjustified.'

The United Nations Climate Conference in 2009 was described by Lord Christopher Monckton, the former Science Advisor to Margaret Thatcher, as a step towards world government[6].

The greatest weapon that promoters of world government use is fear. Through fear people will agree to almost anything. In the next chapter we will see how leaders use fear to implement strategies that societies would not otherwise tolerate.

STOP PRESS

The UN's Agenda 2030 launched in 2015, endorsed by Pope Francis, is a blueprint for world government[7].

Top globalists from around the world converged in 2017 for the World Government Summit organised by the Islamic rulers of the UAE. Significantly the globalists have been meeting annually in the Islamic world since 2013. The UAE operates under Sharia Law and is known for its human rights abuses. CNN and Sky News were in attendance and the UN, IMF, World Bank and other globalist organisations were event partners. Leaders openly promoted globalism, centralised control[8] and a post-apocalyptic vision of the future with humanity nearing extinction by 2050[9]. Speaker Klaus Schwab chairman of the World Economic Forum promoted 'global citizenship.'

WEF is an annual gathering of the global elite meeting in Davos, Switzerland. At WEF in 2017 the brutal Communist Chinese dictator President Xi Jinping was invited to offer his insights on globalism[10].

In the face of rising populism, world government marches on, and with every step it exposes its true tyrannical identity.

Chapter 4

CREATING A CLIMATE OF FEAR

'You never let a serious crisis go to waste ... it's an opportunity to do things you think you could not do before.' [1]

Rahm Emanuel, former Chief of Staff to President Obama

George Hegel, a German Philosopher, 1770-1831, produced what we know as the Hegelian Dialectic, that is being used by globalist architects.

- **Step 1.** **The Thesis.** Manufacture/exploit a *problem* such as war, terrorism, climate change
- **Step 2.** **The Antithesis.** Evoke the required *reaction* – fear, panic, anxiety.
- **Step 3.** **The Synthesis.** Offer a *solution*, such as in the case of terrorism, enacting laws that give more power to the police, more surveillance etc.

Solutions that would have been opposed are now accepted because of the crisis. A greater dependency on the government is being forged. People think they are being set free when in fact they are being enslaved.

The Euro Crisis

The media proclaimed that the collapse of the Euro was

imminent. This would lead to the collapse of the EU that would be catastrophic for member nations and the world. Fear caused an even deeper integration of the member states. They have given up yet more sovereignty in an effort to avert a 'global catastrophe'.

Climate Change

We are warned that our actions are threatening the existence of planet earth. So a Treaty to reduce carbon emissions has been produced out of fear rather than reasoned debate. So even more power has gone to global centralisation.

Terror in London

Michael Meacher, former Minister of the Environment, said; '7/7 we call it…it's a very convenient way of ensuring there is fear, ensuring there is control, and ensuring that those who are in the know - and of course we cannot tell you because it is all secret - are in a position of extreme power.'[2]

STOP PRESS

In an effort to quell the populist revolution a strategy of fear is being employed.

Fearmongering stories abound in the mainstream media: Britain's exit from the EU could spark World War Three, an economic crash, job loss, rising food prices, vulnerability to terrorism etc.

We were told much the same would happen under a Trump presidency, along with Hitler-Trump comparisons and stories of racism and xenophobia being unleashed upon a terrified world.

Chapter 5

GOVERNMENT SPONSORED TERRORISM

Once the people are terrorised, you can force a police state on them.[1]
Mae Brussell, Journalist

The Reichstag Parliament Fire 1933

The Nazi Party had just come to power. The President of the Reichstag, Herman Goring, arranged a fire that was blamed on the Communists. Mass arrests of Communist Party delegates allowed the Nazis to consolidate their power.

Operation Gladio

This was created by the CIA and NATO to stop the spread of Communist influence in Western Europe after World War II. Trains, buses and schools were targeted. Eighty five people were killed at Bologna Railway Station in 1980, but the people were deceived that this was the work of Communist groups. NATO Field Manual 30-31 advises how to carry out acts of violence in times of peace and blame it on the Communist enemy[2].

Operation Ajax

This was the work of MI6 and the CIA to overthrow Iranian Prime Minister Mossaddegh and so to retain control of Iran's oil. Around 300 died in the conflict, and Mossaddegh was deposed and arrested[3].

Operation Northwoods

This was a US Government proposal to commit acts of terrorism on its own citizens as a pretext for military intervention in Cuba. This called for innocent people to be shot on American streets and for passenger jets to be hijacked and blown up as a means to an end. President John F Kennedy rejected the plan.[4,5]

Most people are horrified to think that Western Governments could even consider barbaric acts against their own people. Only rogue states like North Korea would do this. Or is this just what we have been led to believe?

STOP PRESS

In 2014 violent events involving protesters, riot police and unknown shooters in Kiev, Ukraine ended with the ousting of its President.

The people wanted 'freedom from dictatorship' and to join the EU. In reality the coup was orchestrated to promote a combination of US, EU, and NATO interests.

Globalist kingpin George Soros was exposed as one of the masterminds behind the uprising according to hacked emails. On CNN Soros admitted his foundation had played an important role in the coup[6].

In 2016-17 Soros sponsored anti-Trump riots, and had ties to the anti-Trump Women's March where Madonna declared her wish to blow up the White House[7].

ISIS was funded and supported by the Obama Administration in order to overthrow Syria's president Assad[8]. Assad stands in the way of a vital Qatari gas pipeline that could see Russia lose its dominance as a supplier of energy to Europe[9].

Chapter 6

DISTURBING QUESTIONS

An error does not become truth by multiplication, nor does truth become error because nobody sees it.[1]
Mahatma Gandhi

The 9/11 Attacks

On 11th September 2001 four co-ordinated attacks were carried out on the United States in which almost 3,000 people lost their lives. But the 9/11 Commission Report issued on 22 July 2004 has been questioned by high-ranking officials.

Former FBI Director Louis J Freeh said that it 'summarily rejected' the most critical piece of intelligence that could have prevented the horrific attacks[2]. Congressman Weldon said, 'There's a cover up here, it's clear and unequivocal.'[3] John Farmer, former New Jersey Attorney General, said, 'I was shocked at how different the truth was from the way it was described.'[4]

There are seven main questions to be answered:

1. Many of the alleged Al-Qaeda high-jackers, such as Waleed Al Shehri, Abdulaziz Alomari & Saeed Al-Ghamdi, are alive today – their identity was stolen.
2. There have been tower fires in Philadelphia in 1991, In Madrid, Spain in 2005, in Beijing in 2009. These fires raged for up to 19 hours but no building collapsed.

3. The twin towers were designed to withstand the impact of a Boeing 707, said John Skilling, head structural engineer for the World Trade Center.
4. Steel melts at 2800° Fahrenheit. A fire caused by jet fuel can reach 1700° Fahrenheit. If the steel did not melt, what caused the towers to free-fall in ten seconds?
5. Evidence suggests that the towers came down by controlled demolition, falling into their own footprints. Eyewitness accounts confirm hearing 'popping' of explosions.
6. Why did Building Seven collapse, when not hit by a plane, seven hours later within just six seconds? How did CNN/BBC both report this collapse before it happened?
7. The late Danny Jowenko, owner of a Netherlands Controlled Demolition Company, saw video of the Building Seven collapse. He said it was professional demolition work and not caused by fire.[5]

July 7, 2005 Attack on London

According to the official narrative, four Islamic terrorists travelled by train from Luton to London where they detonated four rush hour bombs killing 56 people and injuring 700. But Tony Blair said in the Commons that an independent enquiry would take up too much police and security service time. So a Civil Servant compiled a narrative – of course Home Secretary Charles Clarke claimed there was no cover up.

In any event the demand for a Public Enquiry would have been a farce because of the Inquiries Act that became law just one month before the bombing[6]. This Act gives complete Executive control over the terms of reference and the proceedings of any Enquiry. Lord Saville of Newdigate, the chair of the Bloody Sunday Tribunal Enquiry, said he would not be prepared to serve on an Enquiry subject to such provisions[7].

Chapter 6 Disturbing Questions

The lack of clarity about what happened raises six questions:

1. Was it just coincidence or planned that the Inquiries Act would prevent any accurate examination of what happened?

2. Andy Hayman, Assistant Police Commissioner, said there would be good images caught on camera of the bombers[8], but there is only one poor quality image at Luton Station[9]. The CCTV cameras on the number 30 bus had also been switched off.

3. The official report says that the bombs were home made from ingredients readily available[10]. But Christophe Chaboud, head of French Counter-Terrorism Co-ordination, sent to help the investigation, said that the explosives were of military origin[11].

4. Vincent Cannistraro, former head of the CIA's counter-terrorism center, said that 'mechanical timing devices' had been recovered,[12] contrary to the official report. So were the men suicide bombers, or were the bombs detonated remotely?

5. Prime Minister Benjamin Netanyahu was warned not to attend a conference at the Great Eastern Hotel moments before the explosion took place[13]. Who warned him?

6. The bombers bought return rail tickets and a pay and display car park ticket[14]. Suggesting they expected to return at the end of day.

The Guildford Four, the Birmingham Six and the Maguire Seven have demonstrated corruption in high places when they were acquitted. Michael Meacher said that the global war on terrorism has the hallmarks of a political myth to pave the way for a different agenda – the US goal of world hegemony[15].

Chapter 7

THE FINAL EMPIRE

A fourth kingdom on earth, which shall be different from all other kingdoms, and shall devour the whole earth, trample it and break it in pieces.

Daniel 7:23

He was given power to make war against the saints and to conquer them. And he was given authority over every tribe, people, language and nation.

Revelation 13:7

The Coming of the Antichrist

God knows the end from the beginning; so God was able to show Daniel, in about 600 BC, successive empires that would rise and fall. These would end with a leader who speaks against God, making war on the saints and prevailing against them. This leader was also revealed to John in Revelation. He is called the Antichrist.

Mother of Harlots and of the abominations of the Earth. Revelation 17:1-5

The Apostle John is shown more detail of Daniel's vision. The beast has ten horns or kingdoms but also seven heads. These are seven mountains. A woman, the Mother of Harlots, would ride a scarlet beast with blasphemous names on her forehead.

Babylon meant Rome to the early Christians, Babylon being a metaphor for every kind of abomination. Rome was built on seven hills. In 1957 the Treaty of Rome was signed. The European Union that followed divided the world up into ten kingdoms. All over Europe the woman riding the beast can be found, notably in Brussels and Strasbourg.

In 1968 the Club of Rome was founded with Queen Beatrix of the Netherlands and Prince Philippe of Belgium as honorary members. They were both participants of the Bilderberg Group pursuing world government. A Club of Rome Report, *Mankind at the Turning Point*, says that, a world consciousness must be developed through which every individual recognises his role as a member of the world community[1].

The revived Roman Empire

The Roman Empire began to fall apart in the 4th century AD. But Daniel saw that the fourth empire would seem to die, but would be dormant until later. In 800 Pope Leo III crowned Charlemagne as the Emperor of the Romans, uniting most of Western Europe. In 1512 the name was changed to the Holy Roman Empire of the German Nation. The coat of arms of Germany today is almost identical to that of the Holy Roman Empire.

Hitler's Vision for Europe

Charlemagne was further honoured, as the founder of the European Superstate, by Kurt Pfeiffer, a Nazi, who inspired the Charlemagne Prize for those who have been instrumental in forming the European State[2]. Walter Funk, Hitler's Economics Minister, began drawing up plans in April 1941 for a European Economic Community. This is almost identical to the structure used by the EU today[3].

Hitler was obsessed with religious antiquity. In Revelation, John is told that Satan's throne is at Pergamum. From 1878-1886 a German engineer, Carl Humann, excavated the Pergamon Altar, known as

Satan's Throne[4]. This was transported to the Berlin Museum, and a reproduction was made as a backdrop to Nazi Rallies at which Hitler announced the Final Solution, the extermination of some 9.5 million Jews[5].

Biblical symbols in the European Union

During discussions of the draft text of the European Constitution it was agreed to exclude any reference to Europe's Judeo-Christian roots. But Biblical symbols abound. The flag of the European Union was designed by a Catholic, Arsene Heitz, inspired by the woman in Revelation 12, who has on her head 'a garland of twelve stars.'[6]

The European Parliament building at Strasbourg was modelled on Peter Bruegel's painting of The Tower of Babel. Bruegel created his painting to represent the Colosseum in Rome and the Tower of Babel – symbols of rebellion against God and persecution of those who resisted the edicts of Rome. The name of Nimrod, the Biblical builder of the Tower of Babel, means, 'we will rebel.' God defeated Babel by confusing the peoples tongue. The European Union should therefore be warned, having declared about themselves, 'Europe: many tongues, one voice.'

In 1990 Nicholas Ridley, a Conservative Minister, suggested that the European Union was actually, 'a German racket designed to take over the whole of Europe.'[7] He lost his job for this, but now it seems his words are coming true. The Fiscal Stability Treaty of 2012 has enabled Germany to bring countries like Greece to their knees, to get control, before restoring credit. Max Keiser, of Financial War Reports, believes that Germany will ultimately emerge as the superpower of Europe[8].

Giving the first State of Europe speech from the Pergamon Altar in Berlin on 9th November 2010, Herman van Rompuy, President of the European Council, said: 'There is a sense of powerful and ancient forces driving us… the gods of Olympus before and behind us…'[9]

Is he suggesting that powerful spiritual forces are, in fact, driving the EU?

STOP PRESS

In the wake of Brexit, France and Germany call for ever-closer union within the Eurozone[10]. 'A strong Europe in a world of uncertainties' was proposed by French and German Foreign Ministers[11].

At the Munich Security Conference 2017 the EU army was discussed[12]. Robert Oulds, political analyst and director of the Bruges Group said, "Developing a European Union military force…is potentially far more dangerous because at the heart of the EU is an ideology of expansion, more centralization, lack of democratic accountability." Oulds also warned that a EU military force could be used to crush internal dissent[13].

Martin Schulz, former president of the European Parliament and nominated to lead Germany's centre-left Social Democrats in Germany's 2017 election said, "A strengthened EU is the best way to protect the interests of the Federal Republic of Germany…"[14]

Despite the political and economic failures of the EU, lawmakers call for a fully-fledged European superstate. A letter from EU government representatives read, "Now is the moment to move towards closer political integration — the Federal Union of States with broad powers."[15]

March 2017 marked the 60th Anniversary of the EU's beginnings in Rome.

Chapter 8

THE RISE OF THE ANTICHRIST

At the time of supreme peril I must die a martyr's death for the people. But after my death will come something really great, an overwhelming revelation to the world of my mission. My spirit will rise from the grave, and the world will see I was right.[1]

Adolf Hitler

Hitler's Satanic Contacts

The evils committed by Hitler were not those of a madman, but the work of a man consumed by the powers of hell. He was associated with the Thule Society, also called the German Brotherhood of Death Society, which used the Swastika symbol later adopted by the Nazis[2].

Dietrich Eckart, a founder of the Nazi Party, believed it was his destiny to find the Antichrist, the man who would lead the Aryan Race to world conquest. When he met Hitler he said, 'Here is the one for whom I was the prophet and the forerunner.'[3] Alfred Rosenberg, a Nazi Party member, believed that Hitler was possessed with the Beast of Revelation. Hitler was also influenced by Satanist Aleister Crowley and Helena Blavatsky, a founder of the Theosophical Society.

The Hidden Spiritual Nature of the United Nations

Occultist Alice Bailey and her husband Foster, a 32nd degree

Freemason and National Secretary of the Theosophical Society, founded the Lucis Trust in 1922 under the name the Lucifer Publishing Company[4]. Lucifer is the name given to Satan before he rebelled against God in Isaiah 14:11-13. 'How you have fallen from heaven, O Lucifer, son of the morning.'

Many people consider the United Nations as a benevolent organisation striving to protect human rights and to foster world peace. This is simply propaganda, shrouding other corrupt intentions. One of these is occult, setting the stage for the arrival of the Antichrist. So the UN works with Civil Society Organisations, one of which is the Lucis Trust.

The Lucis Trust has an initiative called World Goodwill. Their work is to help in the preparation for the reappearance of the Christ[5]. But this Christ is not Jesus, but rather the Antichrist. As Jesus warned, 'Take heed that no one deceives you. For many will come in my name saying 'I am the Christ' and will deceive many.' Matthew 24:23-26. Also, 'Who is a liar but he who denies that Jesus is the Christ. He is the Antichrist who denies the Father and the Son.' 1 John 4:3. Another UN approved group is the Aquarian Age Community whose beliefs correspond to the Lucis Trust.

The Antichrist of the Bible

The Bible shows the antichrist will be manifest in many ways:
- He will persecute and wear out the saints. Daniel 7:8
- He will be a master of deception … and will persecute and kill the Jews. Daniel 8:23-24.
- He will be a peacemaker – through him the nations will feel secure. Daniel 8:25
- He will rise up and take his stand against the Messiah. Daniel 8:25
- The man of lawlessness: He will come in accordance with the works of Satan and deceive those who have rejected the truth. 2 Thessalonians 2:3.

- The man who proclaims himself to be God: he will sit in the re-built temple in Jerusalem demanding adulation and worship. 2 Thessalonians 2:4
- The counterfeit miracle worker. 2 Thessalonians 2:9

The spirit of Nazism (Fascist ideology) will meet with Islam in a symbiotic relationship. Hitler joined forces with the Islamic Grand Mufti of Jerusalem to exterminate the Jewish people.

Nazism and Radical Islam

Both can be seen to have:
- Dictatorial totalitarian policies
- A belief in a master race
- A quest for world domination
- A mission to exterminate the Jewish race

The Rise of Islam

Brussels is the most Islamic city in Europe. By 2030 Muslims will be in a majority. France has an estimated 6.5 million Muslims[6]. Muslims put Francois Holland in power. He promised amnesty for 400,000 illegal Muslims[7]. 30% of all meat is now halal, what has been described as 'backdoor Sharia'[8]. In Germany 25 million German language Qurans were given out in an effort to place a Quran in every German household[9]. England is home to 2.7 million Muslims. Anjem Choudary holds frequent rallies calling for Sharia law and says Jihad against Britain will take place when they gain enough authority. Islam's end time march proceeds across the Atlantic. Islam is now the fastest growing religion in America.

STOP PRESS

Germany now competes with France for the highest Muslim population. In 2016 the Muslim population surpassed six million.

Mass migration is fuelling the rise of Islam, evidenced by the spread of no-go zones, Sharia courts, polygamy, child marriages and honour violence. Social chaos has followed with jihadist attacks, a migrant rape epidemic and nervous Germans buying weapons for self-defence[10].

Top Imam, speaking from Jerusalem's Al-Aqsa mosque told Muslim migrants to 'breed children' with Europeans to 'conquer their countries' and vowed: 'We will trample them underfoot, Allah willing.'[11]

Chancellor Angela Merkel said; "What we are experiencing now is something that will… change our country in the coming years."[12]

A TV ad encouraged blonde-haired, blue-eyed German women to wear the Muslim hijab headdress[13].

In Berlin non-muslim Germans sang out the Jihadist cry "Allah Akbar" at the Women's March as smiling feminists looked on[14].

The liberal-left overtly side with Islam, as Hitler sided with Islam.

Chapter 9

AMERICA BEGUILED

We do not consider ourselves a Christian nation[1].
President Barack Obama

The Islamification of America

This is due to Immigration Jihad. As the Muslim population increases, Islam undermines Western culture and politics. Mosques in America have increased from 1,209 in 2000 to 2,106 in 2010.

The call to Muslim prayer sounds out over many cities. A leading Muslim Cleric in Egypt recently proclaimed, 'I swear by Allah almighty, I swear, I swear, that the Islamic flag will be raised over the White House.'[2] Even Harvard University, in 2013, placed a Quranic text in its entrance[3].

Political Correctness attacks Christianity

In Seattle Easter Eggs were re-named 'Spring Spheres' so as not to offend. In Ohio a town changed its Easter Egg Hunt to a Spring Egg Hunt so as not to offend. Under the guise of 'tolerance' Merry Christmas has become, 'Happy Holidays', and the Christmas tree has become a 'Holiday Tree.' The Nazi Party also replaced Christian festivals in their attempt to re-programme the people.

Americans have become deaf through the lusts of the flesh.

The pursuit of self has become the ultimate goal. Entertainment is pursued through seeking after pleasure through the entertainment industry in sports, music, movies, television, material gain, narcotics, alcohol and sexual gratification with whoever a person desires. So the Muslim cleric's words fall on deaf ears.

The Church has become muzzled from expressing political convictions.

In 1954 Senator Lyndon Johnson added churches to Inland Revenue Service (IRS) tax code 501c3. It was billed as a favour to the church, but in fact it placed restrictions on them to claim tax deductions on revenues. Churches can no longer speak out against the loss of liberty or the Obama administration in case they lose their tax status. Pastor Chuck Baldwin has taken his Liberty Fellowship out of the IRS tax deduction because, 'I didn't realise the stranglehold these tax codes hold over Pastors....it cannot be overstated.'[4]

So the American Constitution lies trampled by the globalists. The rise of Islam across America is no mistake. It is another opportunity for the globalists to bring America to its knees. The Muslim cleric said the Islamic flag would fly above the White House. A preposterous notion? Figuratively speaking it has been flying for some time.

STOP PRESS

On 9th November 2016 Hussam Ayloush, director of Council on American-Islamic Relation (CAIR) called for the overthrow of the U.S. government.

Ayloush tweeted hours after the election of Trump, "The people want to bring down the regime." Ayloush met with President Obama numerous times. White House logs omit some of those meetings. CAIR funnelled over $12 million to the terrorist group Hamas[5]. Nation of Islam founder Louis Farrakhan was greeted to chants of "Allahu Akbar" in Detroit February 2017. Farrakhan said; "The God of justice has come... the president is bad" but "have no fear because it is "time for the liberation of our people."[6] Farrakhan praised the Women's March in which American non-Muslim women donned the Muslim hijab and Madonna said she wanted to "blow up the White House."

One of the march organisers Linda Sarsour, wants Sharia Law in America and has ties to Hamas[7]. Farrakhan further stated; "I am here to announce today ... the beginning of a brand new reality ... under the rule of Allah."[8]

May 2017 President Trump signed an executive order easing restrictions on political activity by churches and other 501c3 groups [9].

Chapter 10

DECEPTION IN THE WHITE HOUSE

*Barack Obama to me is a herald of the Messiah.
Barack Obama is like the trumpet that alerts you to something new.
Something better is on the way*[1].

Louis Farrakhan, Nation of Islam.

On January 20th 2009 Barack Hussein Obama became the 44th President of the United States.

He was the first President with Muslim roots who sympathises with the teachings of Islam. Muslim writer Asma Gull Hasan wrote an article in Forbes Magazine called, 'My Muslim President Obama.' Commenting on President Obama, he wrote that 'I have to support my fellow Muslim brother' would slip out of my mouth before I had a chance to think twice[2]. Many Muslims consider Obama to be a follower of Islam. Obama even wears a ring engraved, 'There is no God except Allah.'[3]

Reverend Jeremiah Wright, the Pastor of Barack Obama's former Church, describes himself as a 'second father' to Obama. Wright said that he had made it easy for Obama to understand who Jesus is without turning his back on his Islamic friends and traditions. A telephone call to Trinity Church revealed that Muslims who believe in the prophet Mohammed could be full members. It appears Muslims are welcomed in without any need to change their faith.

Obama's Political Philosophy

In his book, *Dreams from my Father*, Obama mentions 'Frank', later removed in audio versions. 'Frank' is Frank Marshal Davis, Obama's mentor through the 1970s. Davis was a full card-carrying Communist Party member who wrote for Communist publications like *The Chicago Star*. It is no surprise that Obama's campaign slogan was, *'Forward'*, taken from his Marxist background. *'Vorwarts'* (Forward) was the name of the German paper that backed Russian Marxism, and Lenin also called his publication *'Vpered'* (Forward).

Cultural Marxism

Italian Communist Antonia Gramsci wrote that the civilised world has been saturated with Judeo-Christian values that must be cut. Cultural Marxism does this by hi-jacking the entertainment industry, introducing alternate and immoral lifestyles as normal with no adverse consequences. So the sanctity of marriage is attacked, crime and violence are glorified, and the masses become bereft of any true belief or value system.

Control contrary to the Constitution

Obama signed the Executive Order 13603 in March 2012 that gave him full control over water, all human and animal food, all transportation, all energy, all construction materials, all health resources, all farm equipment, all fertilisers, all fuels and much more. These powers are to be claimed in peacetime and in times of national emergency too[4]. Obama also has power to order the assassination of American nationals, not only by drones in the Middle East, but also in the USA, despite the Constitution saying that no one may be deprived of life without the due process of law. In 2013 Aaron Schwartz, a loud critic of Obama's 'kill list', was found dead in his apartment, an apparent suicide[5]. One wonders.

Obama regarded as a Messiah

The January 2013 edition of Newsweek referred to Obama's

second term as 'The Second Coming'[6]. A painting called 'Truth' at a Boston Art Gallery depicts Obama on a cross, his head adorned with a crown of thorns[7]. Reverend Jesse Lee Peterson said that 95% of black Americans worship Obama as if he was the Messiah[8]. The messianic and religious fervour surrounding the cult of Obama is quite extraordinary.

The spirit of Antichrist

Not so long ago Hitler became possessed with the spirit of Antichrist. Could this happen again to another leading politician? Biblical Christianity has been marginalised, and an angry spirit is warring against those who try to proclaim godly moral values. Once Christianity is stifled, other ideologies such as Marxism and Islam can thrive. This will open the door for Satan to come and dwell.

'The coming of the antichrist ... will be attended by great power and with all sorts of pretended miracles and signs and delusive marvels – all lying wonders – and by the unlimited seduction to evil'. Thessalonians 2:9-10.

STOP PRESS

Obama's legacy

Under Obama traditional family was devastated by his aggressive LGBTQ agenda.

Obama endorsed gay marriage. Obama forced school districts to allow boys who identify as girls to use the girls changing rooms and showers. He appointed unprecedented LGBTQ proponents to government positions. Obama worked aggressively to normalise LGBTQ lifestyles among children[9].

Obama was the most pro-abortion president ever[10]. Obama voted against stopping partial birth abortions and against life-support care to children who survived abortion[11].

Obama refused to identify Islamic terrorism[12]. Obama quietly sent the Palestinians $221M hours before leaving office[13].

Unlike his predecessors Obama is not leaving. He remains in Washington DC to fight his Republican successor through his organisation Organising for Action. Its website declares, "We're not backing down." Obama said; "I'm still fired up and ready to go."[14]

Antichrist spirit

A role model of Hillary Clinton was Saul Alinsky. Alinsky admired Lucifer and acknowledged him in his book *Rules for Radicals*[15].

Clinton attended a witch's church[16].

Clinton reportedly attempted to conduct séance-like ceremonies[17]. An FBI agent said Clinton is "the antichrist personified..."[18] Clinton's campaign chair John Podesta was linked to depraved occult rituals according to hacked emails[19].

Chapter 11

THE SECRET SATANIC PRACTICES OF THE GLOBAL ELITE

'Outside the city are the dogs. They are the people who follow witchcraft and those who do sex sins and those who kill other people and those who worship false gods and those who like lies and tell them.'
Revelation 22:15 NLV

The Spiritual Powers of darkness

Satan, since the fall of Adam and Eve, has been called the ruler of this world (John 12:31) and the prince of the power of the air (Ephesians 2:2). In order to gain global control of the planet one must first tap into the spiritual powers of darkness.

As Satan tempted Christ unsuccessfully, so he tempts the global elite today. Power is on offer if we will first bow down to Satan. Of course, people are deceived, because 'Satan transforms himself into an angel of light'. 2 Corinthians 11:14.

Bohemian Grove

This secret society operates in the giant redwood forests of San Francisco. They have played host to such people as presidents Ronald Reagan, Richard Nixon, George Bush Senior and Junior. Also John Major, Donald Rumsfeld, and German Chancellor Helmut Schmidt.

In 2000 filmmaker Alex Jones and author Mike Hanson teamed up with Channel Four to infiltrate the Grove ceremonies. Jones writes, 'I was there witnessing something right out of Hieronymus Bosch's Visions of Hell: burning metal crosses, priests in red and black robes with a high priest in a silver robe with a red cape, a burning body screaming in pain, a giant stone great-horned owl, world leaders, bankers, media and the head of academia engaged in these activities. It was total insanity'[1]. Philip Weiss, who also penetrated the Grove in 1989, concurs with Jones's description of what he saw[2].

Bohemia's Owl

Occult expert Texe Marrs quotes from *The Woman's Dictionary of Symbols and Sacred Objects* by Barbara Walker. 'The wise owl appears with witches at Halloween, the Celtic Feast of the Dead'. The Owl is also associated with the Babylonian goddess Lilith, listed in the *ABC of Witchcraft* by Doreen Valiente as the 'patroness of witches.'[3] The Bible confirms this, 'And these you shall regard as an abomination amongst birds…the short eared owl…the little owl, the fisher owl and the screech owl'. Leviticus 11:13-18. The Jews call a night bird demon Lilith that steals infants at birth. The Bible says that those who worship idols become like them, explaining 53 million abortions in the USA since 1973.

Skull and Bones

Skull and Bones are a society of utmost secrecy founded at Yale University in 1832 as a Chapter of a German Society. Entry into the Order involves satanic initiation rites, the kissing of a skull and the shouting of sexual obscenities. Members take a vow of secrecy and are given a secret name. Members are called 'Bonesmen.'

Ron Rosenbaum, a Yale classmate of George W Bush, secretly filmed the initiation ceremony. A woman holds a knife and pretends to kill a person who is placed in a coffin. He is chanted over and re-born into society. He is then removed from the coffin and given new robes with symbols on them[4]. Anton LaVey, founder of the Church of Satan, describes a similar ritual in his book *Satanic Rituals*.

Recent members have been President George W Bush and US Secretary of State John Kerry. George W Bush appointed many 'Bonesmen' to top jobs – Evan G Galbraith, NATO Advisor; William H Donaldson, Chairman of the Securities Commission; Edward E McNally, President of Homeland Security.

Anthony Sutton, historian and expert on Skull and Bones, believes that its members have set up or penetrated about every significant research, policy and opinion making organization in the United States. Moreover, the first Chairman in 1920 of the American Society for the judicial settlement of International Disputes was the Bonesman William Howard Taft. This was the forerunner of the League of Nations that ended up as the United Nations.

We reap what we sow

The scripture says, 'In the latter times some will abandon the faith and follow deceiving spirits and things taught by demons.' 1 Timothy: 4: 1-2.

STOP PRESS

During the 2016 presidential election Hillary Clinton's campaign chairman John Podesta was invited by performance artist Marina Abramovic to take part in a sickening occult ritual instituted by notorious Satanist Aleister Crowley.

An email from Abramovic to Podesta's brother Tony, asked if his brother would be joining them for 'the Spirit Cooking dinner at my place'. Tony Podesta forwarded the email to John asking him, "Are you in NYC Thursday July 9 Marina wants you to come to dinner."

The Spirit Cooking dinner ritual involves an occult ceremony during which various bodily fluids are used to create a "painting". It is meant to symbolise the union between man and the divine and it is also an occult practice used in sex cult rituals[6,7].

Chapter 12

FREEMASONRY, THE ILLUMINATI AND THE SYMBOLOGY OF THE NEW WORLD ORDER

From the days…of Adam Weishaupt (founder of the Illuminati) to those of Karl Marx, …this worldwide conspiracy for the overthrow of civilisation… has been steadily growing. It has been the mainspring of every subversive movement during the 19th century[1].

Winston Churchill

Freemasons are everywhere

Freemasonry is a worldwide fraternal organisation of Lodges that was founded in the 14th century by Stonemasons who built our cathedrals.

Today the Duke of Kent is the Grand Master of the United Grand Lodge of England. In 2011 a national Masonic Lodge was set up by top British police officers. Over 1000 UK magistrates have admitted to being Freemasons[2], despite a Parliamentary Inquiry warning that, 'Freemasonry can have an unhealthy influence on the criminal justice system.'[3] European Commission President Jose Manuel Barroso met with a French Lodge. The Brussels Journal of 2008 reported this as, 'a major event regarding the place of Freemasonry in the construction of Europe'[4]. Many USA Presidents have been Freemasons, including Bill Clinton and George W Bush.

The Illuminati – a secret influence in all politics – a forerunner of the Antichrist.

The original Masons were men of good Christian standing, but they were infiltrated by the Illuminati. The Illuminati was founded in 1775/76 in Bavaria by Dr Adam Weishaupt, a Professor of Canon Law at the University of Ingolstadt. The Illuminati have an utter contempt for all humanity, and had violent plans for the control of the masses. They were abolished in 1786 by the Elector of Bavaria but soon sprung up again, only to be broken up again. Again they went underground, appearing in 1798 in the USA where George Washington discussed the infiltration of the Illuminati into Freemasonry. Albert Mackey, prominent scholar of Freemasonry reveres Adam Weishaupt as 'celebrated in the history of Freemasonry.'

Freemasonry's respectable reputation

Lower level Freemasons have no idea of the sinister background of what they are involved in. The public admires Freemasonry, which is well known for building hospitals, helping with education – a perfect public relations ploy. The great strength of the Order lies in its concealment. It is only when a Mason gets to the 32nd degree that he discovers that the 'Grand Architect' or 'Most High' of Freemasonry is in fact Lucifer – Satan.

The Symbolism of Freemasonry

Albert Mackey, in his book *The Symbolism of Freemasonry*, says that the 'All Seeing Eye' of Freemasonry found on one dollar bills is derived from Egyptian and Hebrew cultures. Certainly the Egyptians represented their chief God Osiris, the God of the dead and ruler of the underworld, by the symbol of an open eye. But although the God of the Bible describes Himself as never sleeping, He forbids any image from representing Himself, since He is unseen. *The Encyclopaedia of Judaism* in fact links the Evil Eye to the demon God Lilith, the Owl deity at Bohemian Grove.

The New World Order

The design of the Great Seal of the United States has the Latin words, 'Annuit Cœptis', (He approves of our beginnings) above the All Seeing Eye. Beneath the Eye are the words, 'Novus Ordo Seclorum' (New World Order). Many politicians have used this phrase to depict a new political order of Global Government. President George W Bush, a great supporter of World Government, looked forward to an era when, 'a new world order – can emerge.'[5] We know from Biblical prophecy that this will be the New World Order controlled by the Antichrist.

The Deception of Global Leaders

When Satan tempted Adam and Eve they were deceived into believing they could become like gods. Today the globalists have been deceived and behave like gods of the planet. This is the ultimate deception. This is the spirit of the Antichrist, who will set himself up in the new Temple in Jerusalem and demand adulation.

'Now the Spirit expressly says that in the latter times some will depart from the faith, giving heed to deceiving spirits and doctrines of demons.' 1 Timothy 4:1

STOP PRESS

In February 2017 the annual World Government Summit met in the United Arab Emirates under the shadow of a replica of the 'Arch of Baal'[6]. The original arch once stood in front of the pagan Temple of Baal. The Temple of Baal demanded human sacrifice. Baal is the false god mentioned throughout the bible. From Baal the name Beelzebub is derived. 'Beelzebub' is synonymous with Satan. Plans are in place to erect 1,000 demonic Baal gateways around the world[7].

Chapter 13

ONE WORLD RELIGION

One of the aims of the Tony Blair Faith Foundation will be that of remaking the major religions...this is also a matter of promoting one and only one religious confession, which a universal, global, political power would impose on the entire world[1].

Professor Michael Schooyans

Global Political and Economic Control

Global control of the planet is being implemented, largely unseen, through political bodies such as the United Nations and the European Union.

The merger of the world economic system is being achieved through the International Monetary Fund, the World Bank and the European Central Bank. The Mark of the Beast monetary system will come through such banking institutions.

Sorcery, Witchcraft and Pharmaceuticals

In Revelation 18:23 we read, 'for by your sorcery all the nations were deceived.' The word for 'Sorcery' in Greek is 'pharmakeia' which means to administer drugs. Strong's Concordance defines pharmakeia as, 'the use of medicine, drugs and spells...then witchcraft.' The appeal to occult powers was to shield the patient from the power of devils. In 2010 the British Medical Association actually likened the practice of Homeopathy to witchcraft[2]. Homeopathy can use a 'witches' brew' of toad poison, hair from a horse, dog saliva and 'paper remedies' where a substance is written on paper and pinned to a patient's clothing[3,4].

The Pharmaceutical Industry

These companies are amongst the largest and most powerful on the planet. 'For by your 'pharmakeia' all the nations were deceived.' Revelation 18:23. The US Center for Disease Control and Prevention reports that nearly half the population takes prescription drugs[5]. The most disturbing fact is that some of the most used drugs like Ritalin are mind-altering psychotropics. Grace E Jackson, a psychiatrist and author of *Drug Induced Dementia*, writes that these drugs cause brain damage in patients. In 2005 16 year old Jeff Weise killed his grandparents, then shot nine school children before killing himself. He was on Prozac[6]. Many other similar killings have been recorded probably caused by psychotropic drugs. But guns have been blamed because it suits policy makers to cloud the issue.

Bitter water from Fluoride

An end time event prophesied in Revelation 8:10-11 is that, '... a great star fell from heaven, burning like a torch, and it fell on a third of the rivers and on the springs of water; a third of the water turned bitter, and many people died from the poisoned water.' Today an international study of a meteorite crater north of Winnipeg, Canada, found that the impact shattered the sub-surface granite allowing naturally occurring fluoride to seep into the groundwater making the water quality in the communities very poor[7]. Robert Carlton Ph.D. a former US Government scientist says that, 'fluoridation is the greatest case of scientific fraud of this century.'[8] Fluoride has been added to water and toothpaste to fight tooth decay, even though there are reports that the worst tooth decay occurs in areas that have been fluoridated for decades.

The Perversion of Pornography

The end time, 'Babylon the Great, the Mother of Prostitutes and of the filth and the atrocities and abominations of the Earth' is manifesting (Revelation 17:5). As the discipline of Christianity is cast off by the masses, so the debasement of alcohol, drugs, and sexual sin take over much of society. Christians are hated for their righteousness. Pornography is now widely available through the internet, and it is of course seductive, leading to paedophile sin. In 2007 a bronze idol called 'Belle' was installed in Amsterdam to honour the prostitutes of the world. No wonder that the Bible exhorts humanity to flee from sexual sin. 1 Corinthians 6:18.

World Peace

The ideology of world peace is the single most powerful tool that will see a unification of world religions. Who could oppose such a grand plan? But the question is, 'at what price?' Just as the European Union cannot work without greater centralisation, so world peace cannot be achieved without world control – and that will be by the Antichrist. He will sign a seven year treaty with Israel but, just as Jeremiah and Paul prophesied, 'when they (the false prophets) declare, "peace and safety", then sudden destruction will come upon them (1 Thessalonians 5:3). The only source of peace is to live in obedience to God. 'If you walk in my statutes and keep my commandments,...you shall dwell in your land in safety'. Leviticus 26: 3-6.

The World Council of Religious Leaders

This Council works with the United Nations to aid the development of conditions to create a more peaceful, just and sustainable world society. It was founded In August 2000 at the UN Headquarters after a conversation between UN Secretary Kofi Annan and CNN Founder Ted Turner. Ted Turner, who is known for his bias against Christianity, told delegates that Christianity is, 'intolerant because it taught that Christians were the only ones going to heaven'[9]. Different faiths cannot exist together without compromising their core beliefs. Included in the Council emblem are thirteen religions including 'indigenous religions' that are in fact paganism. All such practices are condemned in Deuteronomy 18:10-13.

Islamic Jihad

Mark A Gabriel, Ph.D. a former Professor of Islamic History, identifies three stages – *the weakened stage, the preparation stage* and *the jihad stage*. When Muslims start as a minority in Western nations they are peaceful and tolerant. As they grow stronger they prepare weapons for the final jihad stage when attempts are made to establish Sharia Law. The art of Islamic deception has fooled men in high places. Tony Blair says that he reads the Quran every day… because it is immensely instructive[10]. David Cameron said that the murder of Lee Rigby was 'a betrayal of Islam.' However, Adebolajo, one of the murderers, said that, 'We are forced by the Quran' to kill in this way[11]. Quran 8:12: 'I will cast terror into the hearts of those who disbelieve. Therefore strike off their heads and strike off every fingertip of them.'

The Imam Mahdi

According to Islamic end time teaching, the Imam Mahdi will appear and conquer Jerusalem after breaking a seven-year treaty and make it the centre of Islamic world rule. The Islamic Jesus will assist him. Jesus will be the religious leader who will establish Sharia Law. Jews and Christians who do not become Muslims will be beheaded. 'Then I saw the souls of those who had been beheaded for their witness to Jesus and for the word of God, who had not worshipped the beast or his image.' Revelation 20:4.

It does appear as if the Mahdi is the Antichrist of the Bible, and that the Islamic Jesus (Isa) is the Biblical False Prophet. As Jesus Christ warned, 'For false Christs and false prophets will arise and show great signs and wonders to deceive, if possible, even the elect.' Matthew 24:24-25.

STOP PRESS

In his first ecumenical meeting Pope Francis stated that Christians and Muslims worship the same God. He said, 'dear friends belonging to other religious traditions; first of all the Muslims, who worship the one God, living and merciful.'[12]

In 2014, the first time in history, Muslim prayers and Koran readings were held at the Vatican[13]. In May 2016 Pope Francis met a top Muslim cleric. A mainstream news outlet reported, "Pope embraces grand imam at historic Vatican meeting in a bid to bring the Catholic and Muslim churches together."[14]

In January 2016 the Vatican released a video in which Pope Francis proclaimed that all of the world's religions are 'meeting God in different ways.' The video showed faith leaders declaring devotion to their particular god – Buddha, God, Jesus and Allah[15].

The House of One is being built in Berlin, Germany – it will be the world's first building to contain a church, a synagogue, and a mosque[16].

Trumpet Blast Warning Concise and Updated

Chapter 14

THE MARK OF THE BEAST

'He causes all, both small and great, rich and poor, free or slave, to receive a mark on their right hand or on their foreheads, and that no one may buy or sell except one who has the mark or the name of the Beast, or the number of his name.'
Revelation 13:16-17

The Ultimate Surveillance Tool

The Greek word for 'mark' is 'Charagma', that means a stamp, an etching, a scratch or a brand, as when a farmer brands cattle. God warned Israel 'You shall not make any cuttings in your flesh for the dead, nor tattoo any marks on you. I am the Lord.' Leviticus 19:28.

Hitler used an IBM Hollerith punch card machine to tattoo five digit numbers at Auschwitz. This was a dress rehearsal for the end time 'mark' for all people who submit to the system, just as pets are mandatorily marked today in the UK[1].

Microchip Implants – no more cash

In 2004 the US Food and Drug Administration approved a Radio Frequency Identification (RFID) microchip for implantation in the human body. However in 2007 it was found that these had caused cancer in laboratory animals[2]. As John wrote 'Malignant sores broke out on everyone who had received the mark of the beast and who worshipped his statue.' Revelation 16:2. Despite this, in 2012 Scott Silverman, the former owner of VeriChip, acquired their RFID implants for his new company VeriTeQ, who boasted that they were approved for human implantation,[3] since the Food and Drug Administration had amazingly not withdrawn their clearance. Maybe this is because, as Nick Rockefeller said to Hollywood director Aaron Russo, 'the whole agenda is to create a one world government where everyone has an RFID chip implanted, all money is to be in those chips, there will be no more cash...'[4]

A Strategy of Fear and Convenience

The implantable chip is being marketed by feeding on the fears of the consumer. It will save your life in an emergency, it can save children from abduction, it can measure stress levels, nutrition needs etc. They are also marketed for trivial purposes – to enter gates quicker or to pay for things faster. But better than a chip is an RFID tattoo. In 2007 Somark Innovations announced that they had produced a chip-less RFID ink that can be tattooed on the skin[5]. 'If anyone worships the beast and his image, and receives his mark on his forehead, or on his hand, he himself shall also drink of the wine of the wrath of God.' Revelation 14:11.

Mind Control

Experiments with chip implantation have also shown that a person's mind can be controlled by such a device. Professor Joe Delgado showed in 1963 that, after implanting fighting bulls, they could be stopped in full charge by the flick of a switch. Electrical Brain Stimulation (ESB) can also alter moods in people, lifting those in a depressed state to euphoria or provoke a violent reaction.[6] The Defence Advanced Projects Research Agency (DARPA) has been working since 2009 on synthetic telepathic communications between troops in the battlefield,[7] and even how to remove the enemy's motivation to fight. One can imagine the horror if such devices were in the hands of a totalitarian government who could alter a persons mood to commit suicide or carry out an assassination.

The Mark, the Antichrist and the Number – an Unholy Trinity

The Bible shows that the Mark is synonymous with the name of the Beast who is the Antichrist and whose name is illustrated by a number. Walid Shoebat, a former Muslim Palestinian terrorist, has noted that the words Chi Xi Stigma (666) from the Greek manuscript of the book of Revelation look remarkably similar to the Arabic words 'Bismillah'. The first part of this word means 'in the name of' and the second means 'Allah' followed by crossed swords, the symbol of jihad. The Quran in 27:82 speaks of Muslims wearing the mark of the beast on their foreheads. Could it be that the Apostle John saw the mark of the beast not only as a means of economic control, but also identified the religion from which it would come?

The fact is that there is a prophesied programme for global marking of humans. It will be used by a totalitarian global government to enslave the populace, who have been duped by the apparent benefits. Christians are called to obey God, whatever the cost, and so escape His wrath.

STOP PRESS

Implantable microchipping stories abound; Belgian firm offers hand implant chip to staff[8]. In Moscow and Sweden implants are being used for public transport. A Dallas woman opens office doors. A software engineer in Minnesota controls his smartphone. Australians log into computers[9]. The popularity of subcutaneous implants is growing worldwide. Chip sellers say 50,000 people are now microchipped[10].

The number is set to grow as governments move toward a cashless society. In Sweden retailers can refuse cash. It is impossible to buy a metro ticket with cash[11]. The UK's London buses no longer accept cash[12]. Denmark is said to become the world's first cashless society[13].

The EU takes giant leap towards a cashless Europe, beginning with the elimination of ATM machines beginning 2017[14]. South Korea is set to remove all coins from circulation by 2020[15].

When physical cash is abolished, all payments will be digital – today through contactless technology in cards and phones, tomorrow in the hand via a chip or tattoo.

Chapter 15

SURVEILLANCE SOCIETY

Always eyes watching you and the voice enveloping you. Asleep or awake, indoors or out of doors, in the bath or bed, no escape. Nothing was your own except the few cubic centimetres in your skull.

George Orwell, 1984

Surveillance tolerated by the masses

We live in a surveillance society. The nightmarish future envisioned by George Orwell has become a disturbing reality.

People have come to accept this invasion into their private lives. As Aldous Huxley wrote, 'A really efficient totalitarian state… would control a population of slaves who do not have to be coerced because they love their servitude.'

Global Intelligence Agencies

Whistle-blowers Julian Assange and Edward Snowden have publicised the growth of global surveillance. Global Intelligence Agencies monitor all phone calls, emails and internet activity. Richard Thomas, Information Commissioner for the United Kingdom 2002-2009, said in 2006, 'two years ago I warned that we were sleepwalking into a surveillance society. Today I fear that we are waking up to a surveillance society that is already around us.'[1]

1.85 million CCTV cameras operate in the UK making it the largest surveillance society in the world[2].

The Threat of Terrorism

The fear of death leads people to give up their freedom. After the events of 9/11 President Bush passed the Patriot Act that vastly expanded the US Government's authority to spy on its citizens, even if there is no evidence of illegal activity. Searches can be demanded by the FBI from organizations who are not allowed to reveal that a search has been made[3].

Dictatorial Regimes

Dictatorial regimes, like Nazi Germany and Soviet Russia, persecuted, imprisoned and executed their opponents. These included whistle-blowers, religious groups – anyone who spoke out. Today the Antichrist has only to access church databases to have most Christians in his grasp. This was even a problem for the early church who operated underground and used the fish as a secret symbol to identify themselves.

The surveillance grid has been set – leading to the Mark of the Beast – the end game of surveillance. When the Antichrist system rises to full power he will utilize the power of surveillance to its most horrifying degree.

STOP PRESS

The Investigatory Powers bill passed into UK law in December 2016. Jim Killock, executive director, Open Rights Group, said; "The UK now has a surveillance law that is more suited to a dictatorship than a democracy."

Edward Snowden said, "The UK has just legalised the most extreme surveillance in the history of western democracy. It goes further than many autocracies."[4] The bill allows for legal hacking and reading of information from a citizen's computer or phone without proof of any wrongdoing. Even the taxman can get access to internet browsing history.

In December 2016 in the US a bill allowing government to microchip citizens with mental disabilities for tracking purposes passed Congress[5].

Home robots can turn on lights and TV, order pizza, read to the kids and check on the pets. Equipped with an array of microphones and HD camera's the robots open homes to either hackers or government snooping.

Smartphones store voice and other data in the cloud. Smart TVs are equipped with cameras and can capture private conversations[6].

Trumpet Blast Warning Concise and Updated

Chapter 16

TRIBULATION RISING

*Then you will be arrested, persecuted and killed.
You will be hated all over the world because you are my followers.*
Jesus Christ

The Great Tribulation

From all the evidence so far one can recognise a trend towards the Great Tribulation that the Prophet Daniel said would last for seven years. This will be a time of turmoil that the world has never known.

Tribulation Joy

Christians are called to share the sufferings of Christ. Paul wrote that, 'I am filled with comfort. I am exceedingly joyful in all our tribulation.' 2 Corinthians 7:4. Tribulation also refines the soul. So Paul exhorts us 'to glory in our tribulations because they produce in us perseverance; and perseverance, character; and character, hope.' Romans 5:3. All of Jesus disciples went through tribulation and all but John were martyred, along with Bible believing Christians in the Middle Ages. Those martyred have shown joy in their suffering. They have received the Crown of Life.

The Gathering Storm

The catalyst for the Great Tribulation will probably be a collapse of the global financial infrastructure. Cash will be consigned to history, and the only means to buy and sell will be through the digitized Mark of the Beast. People, desperate for food, will be relieved that they can return to a normal life, feeding themselves and their families, quilling any concerns that the payment system is intrinsically evil.

The Rapture of the Church

At some point in these tumultuous times the Church will be raptured, or 'caught up in the air.' 1 Thessalonians 4:17. There is a difference amongst Christians as to when this will be – before the Tribulation, part way through the Tribulation, or at the end of the Tribulation. What is seldom discussed is that the Tribulation will not take place suddenly. The hour will grow darker in the lead up to it. Believers should therefore be preparing for calamitous times ahead, rather than debating the raptures timing.

Signs of the Times

Why do people hate Christianity so much? Jesus explained this when he said, 'the world hates me because I testify of it that its works are evil' (John 7:7). Authentic Christianity shines with the light of true righteousness. In June 2013 Christians sang Amazing Grace in peaceful protest against a proposed abortion law in Texas. Abortionists chanted back, 'Hail Satan, Hail Satan!'[1] There is no mention of God in the EU Constitution, and a EU Directive removed Crosses from Italian Schools[2]. The Ten Commandments have been removed from Government and Educational buildings across the USA[3].

Silencing Free Speech

Although Western democracies proclaim the value of free speech, in reality political correctness stifles Christians from saying what the Bible teaches about marriage, homosexuality or the right for life of an unborn child. The EU 'Equal Treatment' directive makes it an offence to say anything that could be considered as 'offensive' or 'harass' someone else. Christian Concern for our Nation (CCFON) has said that this will extinguish Christian expression in Europe[4].

A Strategy of Vilification

Christian groups are not only being silenced, government bodies are criminalising them. In a 2009 report the US Department of Homeland Security describe a person who is against abortion, against same sex marriage and who believes in end time bible prophecy to be a right wing extremist terrorist[5]. These are branded alongside Al Qaeda and Hamas[6].

Government Control

Hitler's campaign against the Jews started by alienating them from their neighbours. Bible believing Christians are already seen as 'terrorists' by DHS. As they oppose immorality, they will be alienated from a decadent population. Detention camps have already been prepared for a time of civil unrest under the Federal Emergency Management Agency (FEMA)[7]. The President can now, under the Patriot Act, detain people on suspicion of being terrorists, and we know from Guantanamo Bay that this may include torture and psychological operations to influence emotions, motives and reasoning.

It is time to get ready

We have seen the rising tide of immorality and the threat of governmental persecution. Will we refuse to bow down to an ungodly government such as Shadrach, Meshach and Abednego did? Will we expose the immorality despite the threat of lawsuit or imprisonment?

STOP PRESS

The political climate has unleashed a violent hatred toward those espousing traditional morality. This hatred is akin to Jesus end time prophetic warning, 'You will be hated because of me' Matthew 24:9. Abortion and LGBTQ advocates are among those who have taken a virulent stand against those championing basic ethics and liberty.

Franklin Graham, son of Billy Graham has been accused of hate speech for his views on abortion, sexuality and Islam. In 2017 a Vancouver mayor pushed to stop Graham from speaking at the Festival of Hope in Vancouver. United Church minister and homosexual activist Tim Stevenson said, "This is unusual for us to deal with in Vancouver – this kind of individual and this kind of hate rhetoric."[8]

France has criminalized pro-life speech. If a person declares on a website that abortion 'could lead to adverse effects for a pregnant woman' that person could be prosecuted with a two year prison sentence[9].

In Britain a preacher was locked up for hate crime after quoting the bible to a gay teenager[10].

A Christian singer was cancelled from appearing on the Ellen talk show after a video surfaced of her warning against homosexual behaviour[11].

In 2016 90,000 Christians were martyred across the globe,[12] many by Islamic terror groups. ISIS refers to Christians as their "favourite prey."[13] A priest was martyred by Islamic terrorists in his church in France. Islamic State has called on the "soldiers of the caliphate" to carry out attacks in Europe and the US and to target the "Crusaders."[14]

Chapter 17
THE MIGRANT CRISIS

The EU should "do its best to undermine" the "homogeneity" of its member states[1].

Peter Sutherland,
UN Special Representative for International Migration

Through the destabilisation of countries like Libya, Syria, Iraq and Afghanistan the globalists have created the tsunami of people flooding into Europe.

Among genuine refugees many opportunists arrive without identity papers claiming to be Syrian. Serbian border police say 90% have no documents. Frontex, the EU border agency say the trafficking of fake Syrian passports has increased, while customs in Germany intercept counterfeit Syrian passports.

Hundreds of thousands of people have flooded Europe. The vast majority are young men. Saudi Arabia receives none. Instead they vowed to build 200 mosques in Germany in their continued quest to Islamize Europe[2].

In Germany alone approximately 300,000 migrants arrived in 2016, in addition to more than one million who arrived in 2015[3]. In consequence a wave of mass sexual assaults, Islamic terror and the expansion of Islam across the continent are changing the face of Europe.

The Rape of Europe

In Germany the migrant rape crisis continues unabated. In the first three quarters of 2016 migrants committed 2,790 sex crimes – around ten per day according to official reports. But the actual number is said to be at least three times higher.

Police deliberately omit migrant references in crime reports. Police order German media to delete images of migrant suspects captured on surveillance. This makes it impossible for German citizens to know the scale of the migrant problem.

On New Years Eve 2015, 2,000 migrant men sexually assaulted 1,200 women across German cities[4]. In July 2016 migrants sexually assaulted hundreds of German women and children from the ages of 9-79. In Hamburg a 14-year-old girl was left for dead after being gang raped[5]. Arab men hunt women in a "rape game" called "taharrush gamea" (Arabic for "collective sexual harassment")[6]

In Sweden, now dubbed 'the rape capital of the world', sexual assault against women has spiralled out of control. Since the mid-70s rapes have skyrocketed by 1,472%, with 6,620 sexual assaults reported in 2014 compared to 421 in 1975[7].

In Austria a boy of 10 was raped at a swimming pool by a 20-year-old refugee who claimed his actions to be a 'sexual emergency' [8].

Islamic Terror

In 2015 ISIS threatened to send 500,000 migrants to Europe as a 'psychological weapon'. The strategy is for Islamic State militants to cross the Mediterranean into Europe disguised as migrants, according to letters seen by the anti-terror group Quilliam[9]. The plan eerily echoes President Gaddafi's prediction that the Mediterranean would become a 'sea of chaos.'

Europe has since been rocked by a series of Islamic terror. November 2015 in Paris nine Islamic gunmen and suicide bombers tortured and killed 130 people in a mass shooting at the Bataclan

Theatre. In March 2016 three coordinated bombings took place in Brussels, Belgium – two at the airport and one at a metro station. 32 people were killed. In May 2016 a Muslim wielding a knife cried "Allahu Akbar" killing one and injuring three in Munich, Germany.

June 2016 in Paris two police officers were stabbed to death by Larossi Abballa who pledged allegiance to Islamic State. In July 2016 in Nice, France an Islamic terrorist who shouted "Allahu Akbar" drove a truck into crowds. 86 people were killed and over 400 injured. In Ansbach Germany in July 2016 a Syrian refugee injured 15 when he blew himself up. He pledged allegiance to Islamic State.

In July 2016 Normandy, France an 84-year-old priest was killed in his church. Islamic State claimed responsibility. In October 2016 in Hamburg, Germany a 16-year-old boy was fatally stabbed. Islamic state claimed responsibility. In December 2016 in Berlin, Germany an Islamic terrorist ploughed into a crowded Christmas market killing 12 and injuring 56.

After the Berlin attack ISIS issued a chilling warning that 2017 would be the most deadly year for European citizens[10]. Indeed the UK has since experienced a spate of attacks in Manchester and London with a total loss of 35 lives and over 348 injured.

Countless other Islamic-related attacks go unreported and are described as 'not terror related' or the work of 'psychologically disturbed individuals'.

Islamization of Europe

Mass migration is fast-tracking the Islamization of the continent. Otherwise known as immigration jihad – a strategy of Islam.

The Islamic calendar is based on migration – the Hijra, Mohammed's migration from Mecca to Medina. Today Muslims migrate to Europe with the aim of installing Sharia Law[11]. Islamic scholar Abdessamad Belhaj said, "Migration is seen as a beginning of the Islamization of Europe..."[12]

Pope Francis noted the European migration crisis to be an "Arab Invasion", but explained the new arrivals will enhance Europe for the better![13]

Undercover footage broadcast on Danish TV showed head imam of the Islamic Union in Denmark, Mohammad Fouad al-Barazi, admit that the goal of the migrant influx is for Muslims to conquer Europe[14].

Sheikh Muhammed Ayed gave the order from the Al-Aqsa mosque in Jerusalem that Muslims should use the migrant crisis to "conquer their countries"[15]. A Syrian refugee interviewed on Arabic television also spoke of his goal to "Islamize" Europe by converting its citizens[16].

The UK has approximately 85 Sharia courts, run by clerics who support amputation for theft, marital rape, wife-beating, and child marriage[17].

Globalist Plot

Hitler joined forces with Islam in his quest to control Europe. Today the globalists combine forces with Islam to impose their plan for global governance. Globalism and Islam – kindred spirits – both lust for a new world order and the subjugation of the masses.

Together these ideologies war against common enemies – national sovereignty and a Judeo-Christian rooted civilisation. To quote Communist politician Antonia Gramsci, "Any country grounded in Judeo-Christian values cannot be overthrown until those roots are cut."[18] To rule, the globalists must first defeat a patriotic spirit and rid Europe of its Christian heritage.

Despite the seeming chaos, the refugee crisis is in part by design. The globalists who created the migrant tsunami by invading Middle Eastern countries are using it to further advance their goal. It is managed by the United Nations.

The head of UN migration Peter Sutherland said the EU should "do its best to undermine" the "homogeneity" of its member states,[19] "Sovereignty is an illusion" and "borders…are long gone."[20] The crisis is providing a pretext to implement a borderless and thereby a nationless world. Fellow globalist George Soros who commented that national borders are an obstacle to their plan[21], funds organisations that advocate the resettlement of third-world Muslims into Europe.

Soros also funded a 'migrant handbook' inviting prospective Muslims into the EU[22]. Islamic scholar Abdessamad Belhaj noted how the globalists are using Muslim migrants; "migration is useful" for a "borderless, minimal, global society." He said[23].

The crisis is also useful for the continued assault on individual freedom. As ISIS operatives arrive among the refugees the prospect of terrorist attacks increase across the continent. This in turn allows for the spiraling surveillance of its citizens.

Hungarian Prime Minister Victor Orbán described the refugee crisis as a "treasonous conspiracy" to destroy nationhood, Western civilization and Christendom[24].

Italian Archbishop Monsignor Carlo Liberati said everyone in Italy and the rest of Europe will "soon be Muslim" because of the country's "stupidity" and increasing secularism[25]. Austrian cardinal Christoph Schönborn possible successor to Pope Francis warned; "Will there be an Islamic conquest of Europe? Many Muslims want that and say: Europe is at its end … God have mercy on Europe and on thy people, who are in danger of forfeiting our Christian heritage."[26]

The prophets foretold our world would be controlled by an Anti-Christian dictatorship. Today the stage is being set for this new world order as prophesied in scripture.

"And the beast was allowed to wage war against God's holy people and to conquer them. And he was given authority to rule over every tribe and people and language and nation." Revelation 13:7

Chapter 18

WORLD WAR III

'For nation will rise against nation, and kingdom against kingdom. And there will be famines, pestilences and earthquakes in various places'.
Matthew 24:7

Failing hearts

Jesus said that the events at the end of history would be of such a magnitude that men's hearts would fail them. Luke 21:26.

Dr Robert Kloner, a Cardiologist in Los Angeles, said that sudden cardiac deaths were five times above normal during the 1994 earthquake, and heart failure was observed during the Gulf War[1]. This confirms the accuracy of Jesus words. The antidote to this kind of heart failure is the perfect love of God (1 John 4:18).

Natural Disasters

Another end time Biblical passage says that the moon will turn red because of what is happening on earth. Large amounts of dust scatter blue and green light allowing red to pass through more easily. In 2011 a Chilean volcano turned the moon red. Forest fires have also been the cause of a red moon. Revelation 8:7-8 describes burning forests and a possible volcanic eruption. Could events like these produce the apocalyptic red moon?

Manmade Catastrophes

In 1952 the RAF were conducting 'Operation Cumulus' - rainmaking experiments by pouring dry ice and salt over clouds in southern Britain that caused heavy rain. At this time there was the Lynmouth Flood Disaster in which thirty-five people died. Decade's later residue from Iodide (salt) was found in the waters of the River Lyn, and there is talk to this day of planes circling before the deluge[2]. In 2012 Iran accused the West of using weather weapons to cause an unusual drought[3]. There is potential to control the geosphere and cause droughts or storms as part of a 'soft war' offensive.

Poisoning the Planet

A 1999 report of the British Medical Journal said that people at Camelford, Cornwall, had suffered 'considerable damage' to their brain function after an accidental addition of aluminium to the water[4]. Now there are patents for seeding the atmosphere with aluminium oxide to counter so called global warming. Geoengineering is a threat to humanity.

Controlling the Heavens

Controlling the heavens is possible. A US military document, *Weather as a Force Multiplier: Owning the weather in 2025* details the strategy. This will include systems to produce lightning against the enemy[5]. 'He even makes fire come down from heaven on the earth in the sight of men.' Revelation 13:13. So we read that in the end times, that Death and Hades 'were given power over a fourth of the earth to kill by famine.' Revelation 6:8. One can see that the science is now available to make this happen.

Controlling the Earth

The American Academy of Environmental Medicine says that, 'there is more than a casual association between GM foods and adverse health effects.' Animal studies show increases in asthmatic, allergic, infertility and inflammatory disorders[6]. The chemical attack of herbicides in the Vietnam War led to 400,000 people killed or maimed and 500,000 children born with terrible deformities. Monsanto a leading GM producer manufactured the chemical[7]. The Apostle John saw armour plated locusts with human faces descending out of the smoke – could these be helicopters spraying poison to kill people? Revelation 9:1-10.

Seismic Warfare

In 1997 William Cohen, US Secretary of Defence, confirmed the reality of tectonic weapons. The climate can be altered, earthquakes started and volcanoes started through electromagnetic waves[8]. In 2011 Vladimir Zhirinovsky, a Russian Colonel and Politician, said that Russia could 'destroy any part of the planet,' and that '120 million will die.' This new technology involved being able to start a Tsunami[9]. In December 2004 the Indian Ocean Tsunami killed 230,000 people in 14 countries. So one wonders whether this Tsunami was natural or artificial? The High Frequency Active Auroral Research Programme (HAARP) is a joint effort of the US Airforce and Navy based in Alaska. The European Parliament identified HAARP's ionospheric manipulation system as, 'the most serious emerging military threat to the global environment.'[10]

A Nuclear Showdown

The Bible talks of end time 'wonders in the heavens,…and pillars of smoke.' Joel 2:30-31. The Hebrew word for 'pillars' is 'Timeroth' that means 'Palm Trees'. This is a good description of the mushroom cloud after a nuclear explosion. Moreover 'an assembly of great nations' will come against Babylon, and 'their arrows shall be like those of an expert warrior; none shall return in vain' (Jeremiah 53:23 & 9). No archer could expect 100% accuracy – does this suggest guided missiles? A further end time prophecy is that those who fight against Jerusalem, 'their flesh shall dissolve while they stand on their feet, their eyes shall dissolve in their sockets' (Zechariah 14:11-12). When the atom bombs exploded people were vaporized where they stood. A survivor of Hiroshima said that some people's eyes were liquefied[11]. Revelation 17 & 18 says that Babylon will be consumed by fire. What type of weapon could produce devastation like this?

The US and Russia possess around 95% of the world's disclosed 22,400 nuclear weapons[12]. With such an enormous nuclear stockpile on earth it is inevitable that there will be a nuclear showdown. A foreshadow of the biblical prophecy of Armageddon is being played out in Syria today. The nations are setting the stage – 'and he gathered them together in a place called in the Hebrew tongue Armageddon' (Revelation 16:16).

STOP PRESS

China has spent $168 million on weather-controlling technology[13]. Meteorologists from Nevada will use drones to control the weather[14].

In Turkey, Ankara's mayor believes that sophisticated technology could be used to trigger an earthquake near Istanbul to cause an economic collapse[15].

Britain will experiment with GM wheat between 2017-19[16]. A new trade deal between the US and UK could allow imports of unlabeled GM foods and other previously rejected products[17].

NATO troops continue to amass troops in the Baltic countries bordering Russia.

The Syrian war to bring down Assad continues. ISIS believes Armageddon is coming. Ancient Islamic writings say the small town of Dabiq north of Aleppo is the site for the final battle; here they will vanquish the 'Roman Empire'[18]. Notably Dabiq is close to the prophesied battle of Megiddo (Armageddon). It is about eight hours by car[19].

Chapter 19
COUNTDOWN TO THE APOCALYPSE

'Now learn this parable from the fig tree: when its branch has already become tender and puts forth leaves, you know that summer is near. So you also, when you see all these things, know that it is near – at the doors!'
Matthew 24:32-33

The Return of the Jews to the Land of Israel

In the Bible the fig tree refers to Israel. The return of Israel to their land is astonishing, but also a prime indicator that we are living in the season of the return of Jesus.

When Jesus cursed the fig tree for its lack of fruit, and it died, he was indicating that Israel also was fruitless by rejecting Him and that they would perish also. In AD 70 Jerusalem was sacked, the temple destroyed, and the Jews exiled amongst the gentile nations. Their return started in 1917 when British Foreign Secretary Arthur Balfour wrote to Baron Rothschild that he would support, 'a national home for the Jewish people.'

Israel from 1945

In November 1947 the creation of the State of Israel was approved by the United Nations. A few months later, on 14th May 1948, David Ben-Gurion announced the establishment of Israel the day after the British Mandate expired. 'Who has ever seen anything as strange as this? Who ever heard of such a thing? Has a nation ever been born in a single day? Has a country ever come forth in a mere moment?' Isaiah 66:8. Then, in 1967 and in only six days, Israel regained control over the West Bank, Judea, Samaria and significantly Jerusalem. However, the Arabs retained jurisdiction over the Temple Mount halting the construction of the Jewish temple.

The Third Temple of Israel

The Temple Institute was founded in 1987 dedicated to build the Temple on Mount Moriah. All Temple uniforms, utensils, musical instruments, the golden incense altar etc have been made to exact Biblical specifications. Jesus implied that the Third Temple would be built before His return by speaking of 'the abomination of desolation' referred to by the Prophet Daniel, standing in the holy place. Matthew 24:15. Paul also confirms, at the time of the Lord's return, 'that the son of perdition….sits as God in the Temple of God, showing himself that he is God.' (2 Thessalonians 2:1-4). But Paul also says believers are the temple of God, and God does not dwell in temples made with hands (1 Corinthians 3:16; Act 17:24). Jews say the Temple is the only answer for world peace but Christians know that peace can only be found in Jesus. It is also clear that the Third Temple is quite different from the Temple in Ezekiel 40-48. So there is a conundrum.

Jewish survival, Israel's restoration, plans to rebuild the Temple confirm the accuracy of bible prophecy. We are living in the end of days, the fig tree is putting forth its leaves and the countdown has begun.

STOP PRESS

The Sanhedrin has asked Putin and Trump to help build the third temple in Jerusalem. If Trump moves the US embassy from Tel Aviv to Jerusalem, as planned, it could inadvertently prepare the way for this to happen.

When Putin visited Jerusalem in 2012 he reportedly said he came 'to pray for the Temple to be built again.' The Sanhedrin is now calling upon Putin to fulfil that prayer. Rabbi Weiss, spokesman for the Sanhedrin said; "The leaders of Russia and America can lead the nations of the world to global peace through building the Temple, the source of peace."[1]

The Rabbi's statement should send alarm bells ringing in every Christian ear. The temple cannot bring peace. On the contrary the Antichrist will make a peace treaty and desecrate it (Daniel 9:27; 12:11). Jesus said the world is unable to bring peace (John 14:27).

Chapter 20

ACTION STATIONS!

'The only thing necessary for the triumph of evil is that good men do nothing'.
Edmund Burke

The Days of Noah

Over 4,300 years ago God destroyed the earth in the great flood. Before He did so he warned people of coming judgement by the construction of the Ark that took more than 100 years to complete. But the people mocked Noah, just as they mock believers today. Jesus prophesied, 'As it was in the days of Noah, so it will be at the coming of the Son of Man.' Matthew 24:37.

Some Signs of the End

The question is whether people will notice the signs and repent, or will they perish as they did in the days of Noah? Consider some of the signs mentioned in this book:

- The deception of the masses through propaganda techniques.
- World government through the United Nations and Europe (The Roman Empire restored).
- A world bank born from an economic crisis leading to a cashless society.

- Increasing persecution of Christians.
- The involvement of world leaders in satanic practices.
- The rebirth of Israel.

Commitment not Compromise

If you are someone who has not yet submitted your life to Jesus Christ, now would be a good time to do so. If you are a Christian check your life before God. We should not be lukewarm – consumed with earthly cares – or Jesus will spit us out (Revelation 3:16). Jesus lovingly beckons us to open the door of our lives to continually eat a meal together as friends (Revelation 3:20). Without this kind of relationship we are wretched, poor, blind and naked (Revelation 3:17) only those who win in life will sit enthroned with Jesus. (Revelation 3:21).

Protest not Passivity

As our world becomes darker we must act. Inaction is not neutrality; it is complicity with the Antichrist system. God is looking for those who will stand up fearlessly despite certain persecution. Where are the William Wilberforce's standing against the enslaving power of the Antichrist spirit today? Are we content to live under the shadow of global governance and its surveillance nightmare leading to the mark of the beast? Do we sit in silence or fearlessly run to the battle? It is time to be bold and to stand against the system like Moses, Esther, Daniel, the wise men from the East, John the Baptist and Jesus Christ. Who will we obey God or the Antichrist system?

Chapter 21

WE WILL NOT FEAR!

'My loving kindness and my fortress, my high tower and my deliverer, my shield and the one in whom I take refuge.'
Psalm 144:2

If there is one thought that I would like to leave with every believer reading this book, it would be this: Do not be afraid.

What I have written may be alarming, but we are told not to be afraid even when the mountains fall into the heart of the sea (Psalm 46). We are also told that nothing can separate us from the love of God in Christ Jesus our Lord (Romans 8:39).

We can observe global events with eager anticipation as evidence of the imminent return of Jesus Christ. In that day there will be no more death, sorrow or crying and no more pain (Revelation 21:4). In the meantime, let us remember that even though the nations rage and Kingdoms are shaken the Lord of Hosts is with us; the God of Jacob is our refuge (Psalm 46).

The heroes of faith knew how to live under the shadow of the Most High. Shadrach, Meshach and Abednego dared to defy King Nebuchadnezzar and were delivered by Jesus from the fiery furnace. Daniel was thrown to the lions but the Lord delivered him. Stephen was stoned to death but saw a vision of Jesus and cried out, 'Lord, do not charge them with this sin.' Acts 7:60. All these men proclaimed and experienced, at the height of persecution, 'We will not fear!'

Our prayer today

'Lord Jesus, I come before you now, and acknowledge that you are the God of refuge.

I thank you for being my strong tower of protection in every difficult situation I face.

Enable me Lord, through the power of your Holy Spirit, to live in this reality every day of my life, in Jesus name, Amen.'

NOTES

Chapter 2
1. R W Jepson, *Clear Thinking* (Longmans, 1936)
2. James Sandrolini, *Propaganda: The Art of War*
3. Barrie Zwicker, *Towers of Deception: The Media Cover-Up of 9/11* (New Society Publisher; Pap/DVD, 2006)
4. *BBC 'Is £3M Brussels Propaganda Arm'* (Daily Express, 3 February, 2012)
5. Blanche Johnson, *Trump-themed Hollywood projects are taking over,* (Fox News Entertainment, 17 February 2017)

Chapter 3
1. Daniel Estulin, *The True Story of The Bilderberg Group,* (Trine Day, 2009), 83
2. Daniel Estulin, *The True Story of The Bilderberg Group,* (Trine Day, 2009), 41-43
3. Andrew Rettman, *'Jury's out' on future of Europe, EU doyen says* (EU Observer, 16 March 2009)
4. Robert A. Pastor, *Toward A North American Community, Lessons from the Old Order for the New* (Peterson Institute, 2001)
5. *North American leaders show unity,* (BBC, 23 March 2005)
6. *Lord Christopher Monckton Speaking in St. Paul* (Minnesota Free Market Institute, YouTube Channel, 15 October 2009)
7. Jim Hoft, *Pope Francis Endorses UN's Marxist 2030 Agenda Project in Support of Global Wealth Redistribution,* (The Gateway Pundit, September 27 2015)
8. Alex Newman, *At "World Government Summit," Top Globalists Drop The Mask,* (The New American, 17 February 2017)
9. Zoe Hodgson, *Dubai's crazy, apocalyptic vision for the future,* (News.com.au, 16 February 2017)
10. Sam Dean, *Davos 2017: Chinese leader Xi Jinping says there will be 'no winners' in a trade war as World Economic Forum begins,* (The Telegraph, 17 January 2017)

Chapter 4
1. *A 40-Year Wish List,* (The Wall Street Journal, 28 January 2009)
2. *Terrorstorm – A History of Government Sponsored Terrorism* (Disinformation, 2006)

Chapter 5
1. *Terrorstorm – A History of Government Sponsored Terrorism* (Disinformation, 2006)
2. Daniele Ganser, NATO's Secret Armies: Operation GLADIO and Terrorism in Western Europe (Contemporary Security Studies), (Routledge, 2004)
3. Stephen Kinzer, *All the Shah's Men: An American Coup and the Roots of Middle East Terror,* (John Wiley & Sons, 2008)
4. *Pentagon Proposed Pretexts for Cuba Invasion in 1962,* (The National Security Archives)
5. David Ruppe, *U.S. Military Wanted to Provoke War With Cuba,* (ABC News, 1 May 2001)

6. Fareed Zakaria GPS, *Sino-Russian Gas Deal Signed; Ukraine Picks New President; Interview with George Soros; The Power of Liberal Arts Education*, (CNN, Transcripts, Aired May 2014)
7. Feliks Garcia, *Women's March: Madonna said she thought about 'blowing up White House' but 'chose love' instead*, (Independent, 21 January 2017)
8. Tyler Durden, *Congresswoman Who Says U.S. Funds ISIS Just Got Back from Syria: Here's What She Found*, (ZeroHedge, 31 January 2017)
9. Charis Chang, *Is the fight over a gas pipeline fuelling the world's bloodiest conflict?*, (News.com.au, 2 December 2015)

Chapter 6

1. Mahatma Gandhi, *All Men are Brothers: Autobiographical Reflections*, (Continuum, 2005), 72
2. *Louis Freeh Charges 9/11 Commission Cover-Up*, (Newsmax.com, 17 November 2005)
3. *Louis Freeh Charges 9/11 Commission Cover-Up*, (Newsmax.com, 17 November 2005)
4. Dan Eggen, *9/11 Panel Suspected Deception by Pentagon*, (Washington Post, 2 August 2006)
5. David Ray Griffin, *The 9/11 Commission Report: Omissions and Distortions* (Olive Branch Press, 2005)
6. *The Inquiries Act 2005*, (www.publicinquiries.org)
7. Jason Beer QC, *Public Enquiries*, (OUP Oxford, 2001), 25
8. Jeff Edwards, Chris Hughes, *Mirror, Exclusive: The Hunt*, (Mirror, 9 July 2005)
9. Sue Reid, *Conspiracy fever: As rumours swell that the government staged 7/7, victims' relatives call for a proper inquiry*, (Mail Online, July 2009)
10. *Report of the Official Account of the Bombings in London on 7th July 2005*, (National Archives, official-documents.gov.uk, The Stationery Office, 11 May 2006), 23
11. Jason Bennetto, *Explosives used in bombs 'was of military origin'*, (The Independent, 12 July 2005)
12. Hugh Muir and Rosie Cowan, *Four bombs in 50 minutes – Britain suffers its worst-ever terror attack*, (The Guardian, 8 July 2005)
13. *J7: The July 7th Truth Campaign*, (http://www.julyseventh.co.uk/7-7-liverpool-street-aldgate.html
14. *Exclusive: Was it Suicide?* (Mirror, 16 July 2005)
15. Michael Meacher, *This war on terrorism is bogus*, (The Guardian, 6 September 2003)

Chapter 7

1. Mihaljo Mesarovic, Eduard Pestel, *Mankind at the Turning Point*, (Dutton Books, 1976)
2. *Why the Charlemagne Prize goes to the pope this year* (Deutsche Welle, 2 May 2016)
3. Neil Hamilton, *Germans Push EU to the Brink*, (Express, November 2011)

Notes

4. Karl Humann, *German Archaeologist* (Encyclopedia Britannica, 20 July 1998)
5. Sidney Kirkpatrick, *Hitler's Holy Relics: A True Story of Nazi Plunder and the Race to Recover the Crown Jewels of the Holy Roman Empire*, (Simon & Schuster, 2011)
6. *A More Secular Europe, Divided by the Cross*, (The New York Times, 17 June 2013)
7. Chris Moncrieff, *The EU: 'A German racket designed to take over the whole of Europe'* (Daily Mail, 21 November 2011)
8. Max Keiser, *Germany strangling other EU economies*, (Financial War Reports, 4 September 2012)
9. *A Curtain went up – Ein Vorhang ging auf, President Herman Van Rompuy pronounces the first Berliner Europa-Rede, Berlin*, (9 November 2010, www.consilium.europa.eu)
10. *EU founders speak of possible 'multispeed' future after Brexit*, (Reuters, February 3 2017)
11. *German, French ministers plan for 'strong Europe in uncertain world'*, (Reuters, June 3 26 2016)
12. *Idea of EU Army Signifies Dawn of Europe's New Foreign Policy Concept*, (Sputnik, 21 February 2017)
13. *EU Army is 'a Bigger Threat to People in Europe and Beyond'*, (Sputnik, 2 February 2017)
14. *A Stronger Europe means a stronger Germany*, (Euronews, January 30 2017)
15. *EU lawmakers call for 'Federal Union' of European states*, (RT, February 26 2017)

Chapter 8

1. James Larratt Battersby, *Holy Book of Adolf Hitler*, (J.L. Battersby, 1952), 8
2. Joachim C Fest, *Hitler*, (Vintage Books USA, 1975), 116
3. Erwin W. Lutzer, *Hitler's Cross: How the Cross of Christ was used to promote the Nazi Agenda*, (Moody Publishers, 2012)
4. *The Esoteric Meaning of Lucifer*, (Lucis Trust) (https://www.lucistrust.org/arcane_school/talks_and_articles/the_esoteric_meaning_lucifer)
5. *Purposes & Objectives*, (Lucis Trust)
6. *Belgium Will Become an Islamic State*, (Gatestone Institute, 9 November 2012)
7. Soeren Kern, *The Islamization of France in 2012*, (Gatestone Institute)
8. Soeren Kern, *The Islamization of France in 2012*, (Gatestone Institute)
9. *Germany monitors Koran distribution by Salafists*, (BBC, 11 April 2012)
10. Soeren Kern, *Germany's Muslim Demographic Future*, (Gatestone Institute)
11. Kate Pickles, *Imam tells Muslim migrants to 'breed children' with Europeans*, (Mail Online, 18 September 2015)
12. Justin Huggler, *Refugees will change Germany, Merkel says, as government releases £4.4bn to cope with crisis*, (The Telegraph, 7 September 2015)
13. Robert Spencer, *German TV ad cosponsored by UNESCO exhorts German women to wear the hijab*, (Jihad Watch, September 16 2016)
14. Robert Spencer, *Berlin: Anti-Trump non-Muslim feminists chant "Allah Akbar" at Women's March*, (Jihad Watch, January 2017)

Chapter 9

1. *The White House, Office of the Press Secretary, Joint Press Availability with President Obama and President Gul of Turkey, Cankaya Palace, Ankara, Turkey,* April 6, 2009, (www.whitehouse.gov)
2. Cheryl K. Chumley, *Cleric in Egypt vows: 'Islamic flag will be raised above the White House',* (The Washington Times, 29 March 2013)
3. Neil Macfarquhar, *At Harvard, Students' Muslim Traditions Are a Topic of Debate,* (New York Times, 21 March 2008)
4. Pastor Chuck Baldwin speaks – The 501c3 Government Takeover of the Church, liberty Fellowship of Kalispell, Montana
5. *Trump alert! U.S. Muslim leader seeks your overthrow,* (World Net Daily, December 18 2016)
6. *Farrakhan Enters To Chants Of 'Allahu Akbar,' Delivers Anti-American Speech In Detroit,* (Western Journalism, February 21 2017)
7. *Organizer For DC Women's March, Linda Sarsour Is Pro Sharia Law with Ties To Hamas,* (Gateway Pundit, January 21 2017)
8. Kyle Olson, *Thousands chant 'Allahu Akbar' for Farrakhan in Detroit,* (The American Mirror, February 20 2017)
9. *Presidential Executive Order Promoting Free Speech and Religious Liberty,* (The White House, May 4, 2017

Chapter 10

1. Anne Broache, *'Obama: No warrantless wiretaps if you elect me'* (CNET, 8 January 2008)
2. Asma Gull Hasan Forbes, *My Muslim President Obama,* (Forbes, 25 February 2009)
3. Jerome R. Corsi, *Obama's Ring: 'There is no god but Allah',* (World Net Daily, 10 October 2012)
4. *Obama's Plan To Seize Control Of Our Economy And Our Lives,* (Forbes, 29 April 2012)
5. Kevin Barrett, *Is Obama killing "kill list" critics?,* (Veterans Today, 13 January 2013)
6. *Newsweek Inauguration Special – The Second Coming Of Obama,* (Lonely Conservative, 19 January 2013)
7. Todd Starnes, *Painting Depicts Obama as Crucified Christ,* (Fox News, 26 November 2012)
8. Yasmine Hafiz, *Boy Prays To And For Obama,* (Huffington Post, 14 August 2013)
9. *5 Things President Obama Has Done to Destroy America,* (Charisma News, 10 November 2015)
10. Kristan Hawkins, *President Barack Obama's Shameful Legacy on Abortion,* (Life News, January 13 2016)
11. S. Noble, *Obama's Extreme Position on Abortion Includes Post-Birth Abortions,* (Independent Sentinel, August 25 2012)
12. *Barack Obama used last hours in office to send $221m to the Palestinian Authority,* (Independent, January 24 2017)

13. *Obama sent Palestinians $221M hours before leaving office,* (Associated Press, January 24 2017)
14. Paul Sperry, *How Obama is scheming to sabotage Trump's presidency,* (New York Post, February 11 2017)
15. *Carson: Clinton role model 'acknowledges Lucifer',* (The Washington Post, July 19 2016)
16. Adan Salazar, *Hillary 'Regularly' Attended Witch's Church, Clinton Insider Claims,* (InfoWars, November 4 2016)
17. Jessilyn Justice, *Does Anyone Remember Hillary Clinton's Seance-Like Encounters With the Late Eleanor Roosevelt?* (Charisma News, 8 March 2016)
18. Tyler Durden, *FBI Agents: Hillary Is The "Antichrist Personified",* (ZeroHedge, November 3 2016)
19. Tyler Durden, *"Spirit Cooking": Wikileaks Publishes Most Bizarre Podesta Email Yet,* (ZeroHedge, November 5 2017)

Chapter 11

1. *Occult Activities at the Elite Bohemian Grove in Northern California Exposed! Alex Jones Tells His Story,* (InfoWars)
2. Philip Weiss, *Masters of the Universe Go to Camp: Inside the Bohemian Grove,* (Spy Magazine, November 1989), 59-76
3. Mike Hanson, *Bohemian Grove: Cult of Conspiracy,* (Rivercrest Publishing, 2012)
4. Rebecca Leung, *Skull and Bones,* (CBS News, 11 February 2009)
5. Wikileaks, https://wikileaks.org/podesta-emails/emailid/15893
6. Mike Cernovich, *Podesta Spirit Cooking Emails Reveal Clinton's Inner Circle as Sex Cult with Connections to Human Trafficking,* (Danger & Play November 3 2016)

Chapter 12

1. Charles G. Finney, *The Character, Claims And Practical Workings of Freemasonry 1869*
2. *UK Politics, Tally of Freemason Judges Revealed,* (BBC News, 10 November 1998)
3. *Freemasons in the police leading the attack on David Cameron's riot response,* (The Telegraph, 20 August 2011)
4. *Masonic Influence in the EU,* (The Brussels Journal, 17 April 2011)
5. Andrew Glass, *President Bush responds to Iraqi invasion of Kuwait, Sept. 11, 1990,* (Politico, 11 September, 2009)
6. Photograph with Christine Largarde, IMF, Irena Bokova, UNESCO and others stand under the arch replica. (The Gulf Today, February 13 2017)
7. *At "World Government Summit," Top Globalists Drop The Mask,* (The New American, February 17 2017)

Chapter 13

1. *The World Council of Religious Leaders, The Millennium World Peace Summit of Religious and Spiritual Leaders* (www.millenniumpeacesummit.org)

2. Laura Donnelly, *Homeopathy Is Witchcraft, Say Doctors*, (The Telegraph, 15 May 2010)
3. *Alternative Medicine or Witchcraft? Europeans Cast Critical Eye on Homeopathy*, (Spiegel, 16 July 2010)
4. *Homeopathic Remedies*, (News Medical)
5. *Use of ADHD drugs 'increases by 50% in six years'*, (BBC News, 13 August 2013)
6. *Virginia Tech Aftermath: Did Legal Drugs Play a Role in the Massacre?*, (The Huffington Post, 19 April 2007)
7. *Ancient meteorite causing modern problems*, (Canwest News Service, 29 January 2008)
8. Barry Groves, *Fluoride: Drinking Ourselves to Death?*, (Newleaf, 2001)
9. David Limbaugh, *Persecution: How Liberals are Waging War Against Christianity* (Harper Perennial, 2004), 269
10. *I read the Holy Quran everday: Tony Blair*, (The Express Tribune, 13 June 2011)
11. Ezra Levant, *Multiculturalism doesn't work*, (Toronto Sun, May 25 2013)
12. *Full text of Pope Francis's address to religious leaders*, (Catholic Herald, March 30 2013)
13. *Islamic prayers to be held at the Vatican*, (Al Arabiya, June 4 2014)
14. Corey Charlton, *Pope embraces grand imam at historic Vatican meeting in a bid to bring the Catholic and Muslim churches together*, (Mail Online, May 23 2016)
15. Elise Harris, *In first prayer video, Pope stresses interfaith unity: 'We are all children of God'* (Catholic News Agency, January 2016)
16. www.house-of-one.org

Chapter 14
1. *Compulsory dog microchipping comes into effect*, (6 April 2016, Gov.uk)
2. Todd Lewan, *Chip Implants Linked to Animal Tumors*, (The Associated Press, 8 September 2007)
3. www.veriteqcorp.com
4. *Reflections and Warnings – An Interview with Aaron Russo*, (InfoWars)
5. *Chipless RFID Ink: Somark Innovations Announces Successful Animal Tests Of Biocompatible Chipless RFID Ink In Cattle And Laboratory Rats*, (RFID Solutions Online, 11 January 2007)
6. Jose M. Delgado, *Physical Control of the Mind: Toward a Psychocivilized Society*, (Harper Collins, 1969)
7. *Emerging Cognitive Neuroscience and Related Technologies. Committee on Military and Intelligence Methodology for Emergent* (National Academies Press (US); 2008)
8. Tim Collins, *Would YOU let your boss implant you with a microchip? Belgian firm offers to turn staff into cyborgs to replace ID cards*, (Mail Online, February 8 2017)
9. *Australia Becomes First Country To Begin Microchipping Its Population. RFID Implants in the Human Body*, (Global Research, October 4 2017)
10. Svetlana Arkhangelskaya, *Russian cyborgs among us: technology that literally gets under your skin*, (Russia Beyond The Headlines, February 2 2017)

11. Jon Henley, *Sweden leads the race to become cashless society,* (The Guardian, 4 June 2016)
12. Loulla-Mae Eleftheriou-Smith, *London buses go cash-free,* (Independent, 6 July 2016)
13. Virginia Harrison, *This could be the first country to go cashless,* (CNN Money, June 2 2015)
14. Martin Armstrong, *The War on Cash – One Giant Leap Forward For Government,* (Armstrong Economics, December 5 2016)
15. Bryan Harris and Kang Buseong, *South Korea to kill the coin in path towards 'cashless society',* (Financial Times, December 1 2016)

Chapter 15

1. *Waking up to a surveillance society,* (Information Commissioners Office, Press Release, 2 November 2006)
2. *Top 5 cities with the largest surveillance camera networks,* (Vintechnology, 4 May 2011)
3. *Surveillance Under the USA Patriot Act,* (American Civil Liberties Union, 10 December 2010)
4. Ewen MacAskill, *'Extreme surveillance' becomes UK law with barely a whimper,* (The Guardian, November 19 2016)
5. Congress.gov, H.R.4919 - Kevin and Avonte's Law of 2016
6. Chris Matyszczyk, *Samsung's warning: Our Smart TVs record your living room chatter,* (CNET, February 8 2015)

Chapter 16

1. Tim Stanley, *Pro-abortion activists chant 'Hail Satan!' at a Texas rally. Satan doesn't need this kind of bad publicity,* (The Telegraph, 4 July 2013)
2. Nick Squires, *European Court bans crucifixes in Italy's classrooms,* (The Telegraph, 3 November 2009)
3. Matthew Diebel, *10 Commandments removed from Okla. Capitol,* (USA Today, 6 October 2015)
4. *EU: Free Speech on the line,* (Evangelical Now, November 2009)
5. *Rightwing Extremism: Current Economic and Political Climate Fuelling Resurgence in Radicalization and Recruitment,* (US Department of Homeland Security, 2009)
6. *Army Labelled Evangelicals as Religious Extremists,* (Fox News)
7. Bob Unruh, *Why is the National Guard Recruiting for 'Internment Cops',* (World Net Daily, 7 August 2009)
8. Farrah Merali, *Local Christian leaders don't want evangelist Franklin Graham speaking in Vancouver,* (CBC News, February 20 2017)
9. Steve Byas, *France Criminalizes Pro-Life Speech,* (The New American, February 21 2017)
10. *Preacher locked up for hate crime after quoting the Bible to gay teenager,* (The Telegraph, February 5 2017)
11. *Ellen DeGeneres bans Kim Burrell after homophobic comments,* (BBC, January 4 2017)

12. *1 Christian killed for their faith every 6 minutes in 2016 – study*, (RT, December 29 2016)
13. *ISIS targets Egypt's Christians as its 'favorite prey'*, (New York Post, February 20 2017)
14. Ilan Evyatar, *Islamic State's first act of war on European Christianity*, (The Jerusalem Post, July 26 2016)

Chapter 17
1. Brian Wheeler, *EU should 'undermine national homogeneity' says UN migration chief*, (BBC, June 21 2012)
2. Scott Greer, *Why Isn't Saudi Arabia Taking In Any Refugees?* (Daily Caller, 15 September 2015)
3. Soeren Kern, *The Islamization of Germany in 2016*, (Gatestone Institute, 2 January 2017)
4. Rick Noack, *2,000 men 'sexually assaulted 1,200 women' at Cologne New Year's Eve party*, (Independent, 11 January 2016)
5. Tyler Durden, *Germany's Migrant Rape Crisis: Where Is The Public Outrage?* (ZeroHedge, 27 October 2016)
6. *Muslims Hunt Women In 'Rape Game'*, (World Net Daily, 13 February 2017)
7. Selwyn Duke, *Cover-up: The Swedish Left's Sacrifice of Women to Political Correctness*, (The New American, 18 February 2015)
8. Gareth Davies, *Iraqi refugee who raped a 10-year-old boy at a swimming pool in a 'sexual emergency' has his conviction overturned because the Austrian court 'didn't prove he realised the boy was saying no'*, (Mail Online, October 21 2016)
9. Ruth Sherlock, *Islamic State 'planning to use Libya as gateway to Europe'*, (The Telegraph, 17 February 2015)
10. India Ashok, *Isis supporters threaten '2017 will be a year of massacre' in wake of Berlin and Ankara attacks*, (International Business Time, December 20 2016)
11. Bill Warner, *Migration as Jihad*, (Political Islam, 15 September 2015)
12. Bianka Speidl, *Mutual benefits: Islamic moral economy and Neo-Liberalism*, (Migration Research Institute, 2 August 2016)
13. Tom Wyke, *The Pope says 'it is a social fact' that Europe is seeing an 'Arab invasion' - and it's a GOOD thing*, (Mail Online, 4 March 2016)
14. *Imam på skjult kamera: Muslimer er ved at "erobre" Europa – Imam on hidden camera: Muslims are "conquering" Europe*, (Nyheder TV, 8 March 2016)
15. *Al-Aqsa Mosque Address: Europe Wants The Muslim Refugees As Labor; We Shall Conquer Their Countries*, (Memri TV, 10 September 2015)
16. *Muslim migrant to Europe explains his real motvations*, (LiveLeak)
17. Steve Doughty, *Sharia courts in the UK are run by extremists who back cutting off criminals' hands, says Muslim scholar*, (Mail Online, 28 February 2016)
18. Antonia Gramsci, *Prison Notebook*, (Lawrence & Wishart Ltd, 1998)
19. Brian Wheeler, *EU should 'undermine national homogeneity' says UN migration chief*, (BBC, June 21 2012)
20. *"Refugees are the responsibility of the world... Proximity doesn't define responsibility."* (UN News Centre, 2 October 2015)

21. Nick Hallett, *Soros Admits Involvement In Migrant Crisis: 'National Borders Are The Obstacle'*, (Breitbart, 2 November 2015)
22. Tyler Durden, *How George Soros Singlehandedly Created The European Refugee Crisis - And Why*, (ZeroHedge, 9 July 2016)
23. Virginia Hale, *Islam Academic: Migrants Want Eurabia, Globalists Using Migrants to Destroy The West*, (Breitbart, 14 August 2016)
24. Alex Newman, *Hungarian PM: Mass Migration a Plot to Destroy Christian West*, (The New American, 25 March 2016)
25. *Bishop: Europe To Soon Be Muslim Due To Our Stupidity*, (World Net Daily, 14 January 2017)
26. Barney Henderson, *Austrian cardinal tipped to be the next pope warns of an 'Islamic conquest of Europe'*, (The Telegraph, 14 September 2016)

Chapter 18
1. *Fear can Kill*, (BBC News, 3 March 1999)
2. John Vidal and Helen Weinstein, *RAF rainmakers 'caused 1952 flood'*, (The Guardian, 30 August 2001)
3. *Iran VP claims country's drought is part of West's weather war on Islamic republic*, (Daily Mail, 18 July 2012)
4. Liz Bestic, *Is aluminium really a silent killer?*, (Telegraph, 5 March 2012)
5. Col Tamzy J. House, Lt Col James B. Near, Jr. LTC William B. Shields (USA) Maj Ronald, J. Celentano Maj David M. Husband Maj Ann E. Mercer Maj James E. Pugh, *Weather as a Force Multiplier: Owning the Weather in 2025*, (A Research Paper Presented To Air Force 2025, August 1996)
6. *Genetically Modified Soy Linked to Sterility, Infant Mortality*, (Institute for Responsible Technology)
7. *'Last ghost' of the Vietnam War*, (The Globe and Mail, July 12 2008)
8. *DoD News Briefing: Secretary of Defense William S. Cohen*. (US Department of Defense, April 28 1997)
9. *Secret Weather Weapons Can Kill Millions, Warns Top Russian Politician*, (The European Union Times, 17 May 2011)
10. Maj Britt Theorin, *European Parliament report on the environment, security and foreign policy, Committee on Foreign Affairs, Security and Defence Policy*, (14 January 1999)
11. Tom Robbins, *A-Bomb Survivors Tell Their Stories in Brooklyn*, (The Village Voice, 15 December 2010)
12. Robert S. Norris, Hans M. Kristensen, *Global nuclear weapons inventories, 1945-2010*, (Bulletin of the Atomic Scientists)
13. *China's New "Weather-Controlling Tech" Could Make it Rain on Demand*, (Futurism)
14. Duncan Geere, *Robots will soon control the weather*, (Techradar March 29 2016)
15. *Ankara mayor warns of 'manmade quake' threat*, (Yahoo News, February 7 2017)
16. *Genetically-modified wheat to be grown in Britain despite environmentalist opposition*, (RT, February 2 2017)

17. Colin Todhunter, *Monsanto-GMO Propaganda. "Softening-up" the British Public in Favour of GM Food,* (Global Research, February 13 2017)
18. William McCants, *The ISIS Apocalypse, The History, Strategy, and Doomsday Vision of The Islamic State,* (St Martin's Press 2015)
19. Google Maps

Chapter 19
1. Adam Eliyahu Berkowitz, *Sanhedrin Asks Putin and Trump to Build Third Temple in Jerusalem,* (Breaking Israel News, November 10, 2016)

Unabridged Version,
(500 pages with photos)

Available direct from
www.trumpetblastwarning.co.uk
or from Amazon, paperback or Kindle

In October 1991, Jason Carter received a series of striking visions about the last days of human history. These began with a ten hour waking vision in which he was taken by the Holy Spirit beyond earthly realms and shown things that are to come. What he saw and heard was a wakeup call to the church in Europe and throughout the world.

For over twenty years the only person whom Jason told was his wife. Now he shares these visions and their interpretations for the first time with the wider public.

In this companion volume to his acclaimed *Trumpet Blast Warning*, Jason Carter gives us heaven's perspective on earth's future. Prepare to be challenged. In the world's increasing darkness, we need a brave new church.

Whether you are a believer or not the revelations in this book will not leave you unmoved.

It truly is time to get ready!

Available from Amazon, paperback or Kindle

With Jason Carter on Eternal Radio

YESTERDAY'S PROPHECIES – TODAY'S NEWS

"Groundbreaking current affairs program through the lens of bible prophecy."
Pastor Stephen Merrick, Co Founder, Eternal Radio

To listen visit: www.eternalradio.org.uk

To catchup visit: www.endtimehour.co.uk

Help shine the light into the darkness!

LIKE, SHARE & FOLLOW

Trumpet Blast Warning and End Time Hour
on social media

www.facebook.com/trumpetblastwarning
www.facebook.com/endtimehour
www.twitter.com/NewProphecyBook
www.youtube.com/atrumpetblastwarning

Printed in Great Britain
by Amazon